Brief Counselling: Narratives and Solutions

Judith Milner and Patrick O'Byrne

Consultant Editor: Jo Campling

palgrave

First published 2002 by
PALGRAVE
Houndmills, Basingstoke, Hampshire RG21 6XS and
175 Fifth Avenue, New York, N. Y. 10010
Companies and representatives throughout the world

PALGRAVE is the new global academic imprint of
St. Martin's Press LLC Scholarly and Reference Division and
Palgrave Publishers Ltd (formerly Macmillan Press Ltd).

ISBN 0–333–94647–2

This book is printed on paper suitable for recycling and
made from fully managed and sustained forest sources.

Cataloging-in-Publication Data

A catalogue record for this book is available
from the British Library.

A catalogue record for this book is available
from the Library of Congress.

10   9   8   7   6   5   4   3   2   1
11 10 09 08 07 06 05 04 03 02

Printed in Malaysia

Contents

Acknowledgements

There are many marvellous people to whom we owe thanks for opportunities, ideas, critical comments on earlier drafts and enthusiastic support:

Jo Campling for opportunities, encouragement and advice. Christine Horrocks of the University of Huddersfield and Pat Bastian for patiently reading drafts and sternly admonishing us when we became too bold. Dorothy Jessop and all her staff at Northorpe Hall Trust for their support of Judith on the counselling project and for the opportunities they provided for both of us to work with men who wished to explore solutions to their violence.

Thanks also to Paul Monaghan for his work with Patrick on the Raising School Achievement Project and his supervision of Judith's work on challenging psychiatric stories. We also value his wisdom and creativity; especially his metaphors.

Mary's story was supplied by students who attended Patrick's solution-focused seminars at the University of Huddersfield.

Most of all we must thank our clients who teach us our most valuable lessons. We never cease to be amazed at their creativity in solution-finding. We have taken care to disguise their identities but we have been faithful in our description of their solutions. And not least, we would like to thank Mary O'Byrne for the story of Margot's solution, for coping with Patrick's preoccupation during the preparation of this book and for giving him generous access to the family PC. Judith's dachshund, Rosie, coped with Judith's preoccupation by joining in. She has become expert at making young people feel relaxed.

JUDITH MILNER
PATRICK O'BYRNE

1

Introduction to solution talk

The rationale and plan of this book

While there are many types of brief counselling or brief therapy, this book has the specific goal of bringing before the reader solution-focused and narrative approaches and of showing how they can be combined in practice in what Furman and Ahola (1992) call solution talk. Solution talk is a relatively recent 'wave' in the development of brief counselling, sharing many of the principles and skills of other forms of brief counselling but having an entirely different philosophy and theoretical basis. O'Hanlon (1993) quotes a conversation with Tapani Ahola in which they talk of the first wave in therapy as *pathology based*, where people's psyche is seen as ill or disturbed and this emotional state as in need of healing. The person is the problem and the approaches are based mainly on psychodynamic theory. The second wave covers the main *problem-focused* and problem-solving approaches. While the first wave is also problem-focused in that pathology is a problem, the second wave sees problems more as dysfunctions or deficits of thinking/beliefs or behaviour, based largely on learning theories; or as resulting from unwise attempted solutions that serve only to maintain or increase the problem. The problem is in the person, or the solution *is* the problem, except where family systems theory is used, in which case the problem could be seen *as* a solution in that it is considered to be stabilising the system. Thus it is for the counsellor to analyse or understand/explain the problem and develop solutions, often by teaching the client to think more rationally, learn new behaviours or abandon failing behaviours. The work is often described as brief, that is about six to ten sessions. Cognitive-behavioural approaches and rational-emotive therapy are examples of such work. See, for example, Beck (1991); Dryden (1999); Dryden and Feltham (1994); Dryden and Mytton (1999); Ellis (1999); Feltham

1

(1996); and for brief psychodynamic work, Mander (2000).

In the third wave, the focus moves from problem to solution, searching for seeds of solutions in the client's own repertoire while avoiding a search for explanation or cause – avoiding the need to explain the problem. Here the problem is the problem – it is external to the person and the person is okay – the intention being to begin to construct life without the problem. The focus also moved away from emotions, although emotions are not ignored – they are acknowledged and validated. Insight is also put aside to enable the construction of stories of success and competence in which client goals play a key part and possibilities for personal agency are central. The work is often limited to less than six sessions; see, for example, the various publications of de Shazer and White cited in this volume; as well as the British works of Hawkes, Marsh and Wilgosh (1998); O'Connell (1998); Payne (2000).

Despite third-wave approaches inviting counsellors to abandon expertise in 'diagnosis', they retain many core counselling skills and values. However, the philosophy does shift the emphasis and revises some aspects of core skills. Listening, for example, remains a central skill but what we listen for shifts towards competence rather than deficit; it also seeks to stay on the surface, avoiding interpretations, and watches out for exceptions and occasions when the person stood up to the problem. Solution talk is clearly in this third wave of brief counselling.

While this book is written from a third-wave orientation we do not wish to suggest that second-wave work is not brief or effective. Nor do we claim that solution talk is fundamentally superior to other forms of counselling, although its effectiveness has been well-established (see Appendix 1 for a review of the outcomes research). We write of it because it is what we currently practise and because we find its philosophy particularly helpful. A considerable attraction of the approach for us is that it seems to be less stressful than other work we have done – it can be light, and playful even, as it brings forth the creativity of clients. An equally attractive consideration is the inherently anti-discriminatory nature of the approach which makes empowering clients more straightforward. And, when clients own their solutions, they are more able to meet further problems they encounter. Two brief, but typical, extracts from letters we receive illustrate this advantage:

When I saw you last time, you asked me what you could have done that would have been more helpful and I think I responded by saying I may have liked to talk more about the problem itself. In hindsight, I was wrong. One of the most helpful things about meeting you was that I felt like an ordinary person with a problem to solve and not a client in therapy. This in itself was extremely empowering. You have helped me to change my life in a most profound way.

My pearants [*sic*] really don't approve of me going away at Christmas but for once I'm not going to let them spoil it. Hopefully I've found Mr Right and hopefully I'll stay happy. If things go wrong I'll just do what I always do now and pick myself up and start again.

The theory underpinning solution talk is relatively simple but the practice is not simplistic, so this chapter will outline both what solution talk is and what it is not; comparing it with other forms of brief counselling. Some comparisons with other approaches will also emerge in Chapters 2 and 3, which are concerned with the basic principles and techniques which are rooted in constructionism, with illustrations from our practice. Chapter 4 sets out the detail of a first counselling session and Chapter 5 the general format of subsequent sessions and how progress is not only maintained but amplified.

Chapters 6 to 9 are developed around themes. While we address some common issues such as eating difficulties, we do not offer separate chapters on how to work with specific problems as we are more interested in solutions. Likewise we do not offer a discrete chapter on anti-discriminatory practice – issues of power and oppression are picked up at several points throughout the book. In these themed chapters we present several case examples for the reader's consideration which, apart from the case of Mary in Chapter 8 and Margo in Chapter 9, are from our own counselling practice. We do not claim that the work is perfect or that there is always a 100 per cent successful outcome, having chosen our examples to illustrate the complexities of our clients' lives. We stress that the approach is first and foremost one of philosophical orientation and, secondly, the creative use of some tried and tested techniques and skills, some from counselling more generally, but bound together by a specific set of principles. Chapter 10 will reiterate the underlying philosophy and view of human nature held by counsellors who practice solution talk; re-examining how and why it works. The appendices contain a review of outcomes research, a reading list for those interested in learning more about the approach, and some useful tools for use in practice.

Some aspects of brief counselling in general

In order to establish a satisfactory helping relationship, counsellors are expected to exhibit certain behaviours such as congruence, acceptance and empathy (Rogers, 1961); listening, empathic understanding, respect for the client's reality, and a confidence that the client will achieve reasonable goals (Cooper, 1995). A significant difference between the various forms of counselling is that there has been a shift from an almost professional detachment in psychodynamic forms of counselling, through the unconditional positive regard of the humanistic tradition of person-centred counselling, to a more vibrant relationship that is higher on sharing with the client and showing some emotional involvement in brief counselling (Kaplan, 1992). In third-wave work the relationship is more like that of a not-knowing friend who puzzles with the client over what will be happening when the problem is no more. In this way client and counsellor co-construct the future.

Genuineness is also highly valued although, as Masson has pointed out, professionalising a relationship and limiting the contact to hourly sessions could be seen as reducing genuineness: 'No real person really does any of the things Rogers discusses in real life' (1989: 232). Counselling boundaries, which Manthei says must not be violated and Mearns views as a relationship in which the counsellor knows how to be present and at the same time keep her distance (1994:112), are also expected although more difficult to understand. When does boundary-setting and distance become lack of empathy? Counselling, says the British Association for Counselling and Psychotherapy, is a non-exploitative activity based on the values of integrity, impartiality and respect (BACP, 2001, web site). The intention of all counselling is to have a clear set of rules to protect the client from harm, and ensure the counsellor remains in control. The key difference between counselling and ordinary friendship says Woolfe is intentionality: 'counselling is an activity engaged in deliberately, with a clear intention and operating according to clearly defined set of rules' (1997: 4). Or in the words of the British Association for Counselling and Psychotherapy: 'a deliberately undertaken contract, with clearly agreed boundaries and a commitment to privacy and confidentiality' (BACP,

2001, web site). In viewing clients as experts in their own lives, solution-focused counselling attempts to give clients control over how these ethics work out in practice.

For Culley and Wright (1997: 254), brief counselling is 'a pragmatic approach which focuses on problem solution or management by the most efficient route. Brief counselling does not espouse the notion of "cure" or have character change as one of its goals . . .'. Although it is difficult to compare different styles of counselling because of their different aims, outcomes research shows that brief counselling has several advantages over longer-term interventions. First, it accords with what clients want and expect, particularly the number of sessions. Second, for lasting change it compares favourably with longer-term interventions (see Parton and O'Byrne, 2000, chapter 9), probably because it utilises the surges of enthusiasm, hope and well-being which are present during the initial stages of counselling. Third, having no notion of an ideal emotional state which clients should achieve before they can be said to no longer need counselling, it does away with notions of *cure* and *termination*. Change is not seen as a linear process requiring weekly sessions where insights are gained, rather change may be accelerated at the beginning of counselling and continue beyond it, with most of that change happening *between* the sessions. As change is seen as a continuous, unfolding and variable process (Culley and Wright, 1997: 261), sessions are often widely spaced and follow up, or review, sessions built in on the basis that clients often seek help at different stages of their lives. Most importantly of all, brief counselling does not cast the client as fundamentally deficient: 'few problems exist all the time, and neither do problem reinforcing patterns. Rather individuals are more usually in a state of flux, desperately experimenting with potential solutions' (Wheeler, 1995: 255). That is, they are not cast *as* the problem but *in* the problem or *under* its influence. In the psychodynamic counselling literature, these advantages would probably be construed as disadvantages; the main one being a charge of superficiality.

Much of the earlier counselling theory located the origins of problems in an individual's psyche, seeking always an underlying psychological rationale for problems which discounts, or is suspicious of, clients' explanations. Dealing with 'surface' problems is often viewed as dangerous in that problems might be driven deeper underground. In psychodynamic-based work any resistance on the part of the client to the counsellor's exploration of these deeper motivations is seen as an inevitable part of the counselling process requiring an understanding of the mind's mechanisms of defence. This 'knowledge' explains the addition of developing personal 'insight' and a preoccupation with past events to the counselling role; even though clients rarely ask for this. Indeed, they sometimes find this patronising and unhelpful. For example, Avril asked for a change from her counsellor after three frustrating sessions where Avril tried to talk about managing her eating and her counsellor persisted in hinting of a possibility that she could not eat because she was denying earlier sexual abuse. At her third session, Avril raised her dissatisfaction with the counselling process but was told that she needed to 'work through' her feelings about counselling; thus locating the failure of the counselling in the client, not any possible lack in the counsellor's approach or understanding. Avril voted with her feet and found herself a solution-focused counsellor who worked with her on the 'surface' problem. At the second session Avril reported that she was eating 'properly' and was much happier as a result. Her original counsellor felt that this was 'flight into health' and that her problems would resurface in another form, or that Avril was being manipulative; this counsellor having an 'expert' explanation of anorexia which 'interpreted' any show of self-will on the part of a client with eating difficulties as repressed anger. This is not a problem for the solution-focused brief counsellor who will simply say that these can be dealt with when, and if, they occur.

The style of the counsellor is also different in brief counselling. The counsellor is more interactive, what Culley and Wright (1997) refer to as a 'galvaniser' who is able to form a relationship speedily, and sustain it. This means that it is high on emotional involvement, with the counsellor remaining positive and confident about her expectations of clients' capacities to solve their problems (Cooper, 1995; Dolan, 1998). This style of working is also viewed by psychodynamic counsellors as potentially dangerous; particularly in terms of boundary transgressions and the possibility of transference emerging. However, Ingleby (1985) considers that transference is a highly patronising concept, involving as it does the counsellor offering unconditional warmth and regard but limiting these at the first sign of the client responding warmly. The counsellor, he says, wants the advantage of being a beneficent father figure but tells the client, at the same time, that they must not love this 'father'.

Additionally, emphasising the slow building of a relationship can hinder a focus on the work needing to be done. Client frustration with a first-wave style of counsellor is illustrated with yet another example of a client who changed to brief counselling. The notes on Samantha told of a young woman who was 'dissociated' from her feelings, unable to concentrate and settle to counselling. This counsellor's aim was, 'to continue art work in the hope of building a psychological relationship'. Samantha asked her new counsellor if she liked the picture she had just hastily drawn. 'Not particularly', replied the counsellor honestly. 'You are supposed to say what it means', Samantha countered. 'Well, I haven't a clue. I've never been any good at deciding what pictures mean. I find it much easier to ask people for their opinion.' There was a moment's pause and Samantha said, 'I like that. You don't take any crap. My last counsellor just sat there while I drew pictures.' 'What will I be doing if I am being helpful?' asked the counsellor. 'Asking me questions', replied Samantha.

From this it will be apparent that we consider the brief counselling approach, with its emphasis on the task the client wishes to achieve, a more efficient and ethical way to proceed. All forms of counselling can be brief, and indeed often become brief by the client leaving the process. Psychodynamic work need not necessarily be long-term (see, for example, Mander, 2000) but it tends to be. Because clients determine when they have reached their goals, solution-focused brief therapy can consist of only one session but, rarely, may involve an indeterminate number of sessions.

What solution talk is

As the title of the book shows, we prefer a particular form of brief counselling; one which combines solution-focused and narrative approaches. Our enthusiasm for this way of working was based initially on outcome research which shows that clients over a very wide range of disciplines (as diverse as nursing, police work, and industry) consider it not only an effective approach to solution-building but also painless (for an overview, see Parton and O'Byrne, 2000). More recently, we have been influenced by our own experiences. Our clients, whether they be individuals, families, groups or communities, have mostly met their goals more frequently and quickly since we adopted the approach – the average number of sessions being 3.4. We find that more sessions are needed when social services are involved due to child protection or looked-after children issues. We are convinced that it is mainly the philosophy of the method that is important; the techniques flow from that philosophy. The approach concentrates on solution talk rather than problem talk; we explain below what solution talk is and how it has the potential to avoid the traps of earlier types of counselling.

Solution talk is a combination of two social-constructionist approaches, one *solution-focused*, the other *narrative*-based. The solution-focused approach is based on a close study of what works, how fast it works, and how satisfied clients are with the outcome. A major contribution to this study has been made by de Shazer and his colleagues in Milwaukee (de Shazer, 1982, 1985, 1991, 1993). It emerged that the philosophical ideas of Wittgenstein (1963) and Derrida (1978) fitted well with what de Shazer was learning from clients; namely that realities were constructed by language, that counselling is a language game. The centrality of language in counselling means that listening at the level of the word is the key (for a fuller discussion, see Weingarten, 1998). Looking below the surface for deeper meanings only reveals more about professional constructions of problems and of ways in which they can be resolved, ignoring clients' realities. Thus the pursuit of a 'true' understanding of the problem is futile where psycho-social problems are concerned (in physical conditions, of course, diagnosis is more useful) and what is needed is language with which to construct solutions.

More importantly, de Shazer learned that the seeds of solutions to problems already exist within people and their stories, and that these solutions can be found in the *exceptions* to problems; that is, those occasions when the problem is absent or less of a problem. The essential tasks of an effective counsellor were demonstrated to be: listening for what the client wants, negotiating achievable (and legal) goals, discovering how these were already being achieved in some small ways (past or present), and keeping track of what is happening that is useful and doing more of it. Solution talk is, then, future-oriented instead of being preoccupied with the past, emphasises human resources rather than risks, and studies success instead of failure. It tends to be brief although it is not always so.

This is not to confuse the work with the positive reinforcements of behavioural counselling or the ego strengthening of psychotherapy or versions of Positive Thinking. Because, as narrative theory says, we create ourselves in the telling of our stories, talking about how the client 'did that' and how they can do more of what is helpful to them develops a greater sense of self-agency. It is not always easy to find exceptions to problems – or to get clients to talk about them rather than the problems – so a high degree of communication skill is required if a picture of a possible future without the problem is to be constructed. For example, Sadie was suffering greatly from her inability to cope with cruel playground taunts relating to a recent sexual assault. She longed to be able to 'answer back' but, being a polite and quiet teenager, could not think of a single exception to her submissive response to pupils' taunts. By focusing on her own words – 'answering back' – she was able to identify one occasion when she did manage to do this; when she was required to do so as part of a planned debate in her English class. By extending her classroom 'debating' skill, she was able to 'answer back' in the playground. As she became more confident in the playground, she further developed the confidence to 'answer back' to her parents when they rejected her tentative hopes to transfer to a school where she could have specialist tuition in music. They initially saw this as her 'avoiding' coming to terms with her experience of sexual assault. Her solution has worked well for her as she is happy and doing well at her new school, being more able to put the experiences behind her in a situation where she is functioning well.

If there are no exceptions, the client is asked to 'do something different', the word 'instead' being an important element of the work. If you are getting stuck in your work with clients, don't search for a reason in the client – such as 'resistance' – ask what you would be doing instead if you were being more helpful. For example, Kahn (1997) comments on how hurt he feels when a client he likes gives him three on Rogers' eight-point empathy scale: 'I felt a rush of indignant hurt flash through my body. It lasted only a moment, and then I set to work suppressing it. This is wonderful, I said to myself. I've been waiting for negative transference for months, and here it is' (Kahn, 1997: 125). What puzzles us is why he does not consider that the client may have been right in his assessment? It would have been relatively simple to ask, 'what would I be doing differently if you scored me at four?' Clients do not take the trouble to attend counselling sessions to sit there and be resistive; such behaviour probably indicates a strength in that they are doggedly persisting with counselling in the hope that you will eventually understand them and work out how best you can help them.

The second partner in our combination approach is equally interesting. At the same time as de Shazer was developing his ideas on solution-focused counselling in America, others in Australasia were developing what became known as *narrative therapy* (notably White, 1984, 1993, 1995, 1996; White and Epston, 1990; Epston, 1998). This way of working is more political and social in nature, being based on the sociology of the post-structuralist Foucault (1972, 1973, 1980, 1988) and the sociolinguist Halliday (1978) concerning the oppressive effects of dominant narratives on people's understanding of the validity of their ways of living. White sought to discuss with clients the influences and ideas that recruited them into their problems. His work differs from de Shazer's in so far as he considers it important to deconstruct dominant cultural stories before constructing solutions. He challenges people's beliefs that a problem speaks their identity; what he calls being entered into a story. Clients often talk about this story as though it is 'true', despite traditional ways of explaining human behaviour having been shown to be unreliable (Dryden and Feltham, 1994). This takes account of power differentials, particularly sexist discourses that recruit women into submissive roles or denigrate them. Thus a narrative approach to brief counselling is less vulnerable to criticisms of solution-focused approaches that gender issues are ignored (see, for example, Dermer *et al.*, 1998).

For instance, following a rape as she came home *late from work*, Charlotte told her interviewing police officer that she did not feel able to give evidence in court as she felt diminished by a report in the local newspaper that she had been walking home *from a night out*. Although not named in the newspaper account, she viewed this as storying her as a 'slag'; her internalised story about what constituted a 'slag' colluding with the newspaper's narrative. Believing that as a 'slag' she would get little sympathy for her predicament, she was unable to pursue her original preferred solution to give evidence in court. How life is talked about (storied) seems to be not only descriptive of reality but also capable of constituting reality, with language playing the major role in creating social as well as individual realities.

White considers that this notion contains great hope. When he asks clients about the occasions they had stood up to the problem, and the supporting narrative, there are heroic acts and lives that had been edited out; that had been unstoried and unstored until he asked. By asking what these occasions, 'unique outcomes', say about the client, the client emerges as different and he then encourages them to relate this new story to others, thereby bringing it to life. For example, Robin's disruptive and aggressive behaviour towards teachers and pupils in his junior school storied him as 'dangerous', but, because he suffered from asthma and bed wetting, he was also entered into a psychological story which described him as 'disturbed'. His mother had stood up to the 'dangerous' story by asking to have him moved to another class where he had a better relationship with the teacher (this failed on the grounds that the head teacher felt that Robin couldn't be seen to 'win'), and by challenging the many negative comments in his homework book (this also failed; instead of balancing the negative comments with positive ones – which would have revealed the exceptions to the problem story – the school redesigned the homework books, removing the comments section altogether). Robin's mum then accepted the 'disturbed' story, which she began to believe as Robin was so distressed by rows with one particular teacher that he was unable to eat for the rest of the day or sleep at night. A brief conversation about any possible unique outcomes revealed that Robin had stood up to the story of oppositional behaviour: he had voluntarily taken on the task of teaching computer skills to a boy with learning difficulties, despite this being the source of teasing from other boys who were also generally known for their disruptive behaviour (for a fuller discussion of how boys construct and perform their masculine behaviours at school, see Messerschmidt, 2000). He was surprised but pleased at what this said about himself as a person; and was able to say that it was this caring, responsible side of himself that he wished to develop more.

Strand (1997) suggests that externalising the problem and its internalised narrative in an attempt to unmask the relationship between the self and hidden political realities requires advanced conceptual ability, whereas a solution-focused approach only demands a rethink of the definition of one concept – the problem – without concern for its effect on self-definition. This, he thinks, makes solution-focused approaches more suitable for people of limited conceptual ability. We have not found this to be the case, having used a narrative approach quite successfully with both children and adults with learning difficulties. What can make a narrative approach more complicated is where a person's thoughts are so chaotic that they have difficulty in working out which 'voices' are their own and which are external representations of dominant narratives.

Later counsellors began to combine the solution-focused ideas of de Shazer and the narrative ideas of White, most notably O'Hanlon (1989, 1991, 1993, 1994, 1999) but also Furman and Ahola (1992) and

Milner (2001). They developed many metaphors for the externalisation of problems; a process whereby the problem is storied as outside the person and as having a personality of its own. This enables the counsellor, client and family to join forces against the problem rather than the person. For example, when asked what his problem would look like if he drew a picture of it, Robin described a blue smouldering fire that burst into red flames when a particular teacher shouted at him; whereas Tony saw his temper problem as a red raging bull that burst out when he was frustrated, and Shannon saw her eating problem as a brownish thorn bush all tangled up inside her stomach – although it had a few bright green leaves. These young people's parents all found it much easier to join with their children in their efforts against the problems once they understood the problems' personalities. Similarly, Furman and Ahola find it much more constructive to story 'depression' as 'latent joy', and 'borderline personality disorder' as a 'search for a new life direction'; the latter being much easier to find than the problem is to be lost.

We find that while either the solution-focused or narrative approach works well in various situations, combining them is even more effective. The narrative approach seems particularly important in helping people whose lives are very complex and for whom there is no single solution which will not endanger their social selves. For example, most women's effective resistance to oppressive sexist discourses is complicated and subtle, including refusing to submit to others pejorative definitions about themselves, especially comments on their performance of 'good' mothering; at the same time as holding on to connections and relationships that the problem threatens; raising one's children to recognise both dominant and marginalised cultures; and finding happiness in the dailyness of life (Stacey, 1997). Thus although Cassie eventually broke free from a relationship with a violent man, she did not wish to attend a domestic violence group as she had no wish to have her feminist consciousness raised. Her reality was that many of the men she knew were violent and she wished only to be able to negotiate a 'safe' route through her relationships.

A combined solution-focused/narrative approach has a non-expert attitude; claiming that it is not necessary to understand a problem in order to solve it; that talking about a future without the problem linguistically creates such a future; and that talking about previously ignored exceptions makes them bigger. The focus on feelings is less in that once they are adequately acknowledged through careful enquiry rather than interpretation and intuition, it is possible to move swiftly on to goal clarification. As will be shown in the next chapter, empathy is redefined as engaging at an emotional level rather than seeking to show understanding of emotions; that having clients feel understood is what matters; and a vital part of this is understanding what they want – not what we think would be desirable or what is the cause of the problem. Furthermore, the very purpose of counselling is shifted from freeing clients from their repressions and a drive towards a perfect self, or to meet idealised notions of needs and self-esteem, towards the measurable goal of enriching lives. These enriched lives are constructed by the client, not by attempting to cure deficits defined by 'expert' diagnoses. Diagnoses shut down possibilities as, if the prescribed cure fails to work, the client is left with nothing but a label that merely excuses them from personal responsibility-taking. Enriched lives have greater hope, more possibilities, and more personal agency and creativity.

What is different about solution talk

In our view, the practice of solution talk cannot easily be combined with problem-focused counselling in some sort of 'add on' way in certain cases, as an entirely different set of principles is involved based on a fundamentally different way of understanding people. These principles affect the practice, and we outline below the major differences that distinguish third-wave counselling:

1   When engaging in solution talk, the conversation accepts people's experiences rather than seeks 'true' explanations. Here the counsellor is attempting to utilise the client's 'local' knowledge by asking for as much detail as possible about their description of the problem rather than have a set of explanations gleaned from professional knowledge. For example, by listening to Jack's description of his violent rages and asking where these happened, what they were like, what feelings and behaviours accompanied them, it emerged that they had nothing at all to do with his feelings of abandonment by his father and his subsequent inability to maintain relationships with girlfriends (his mother's insights gained from her own counselling following her marriage break-up), but were largely fuelled by his high consumption of alcohol when out with his heavy-drinking mates.

2   The search for solutions rather than an understanding of problems means that the counsellor has little interest in asking 'why' questions. Not only can previous poor experiences not be changed, but understanding why something happened does not necessarily lead to problem resolution. What understanding problems does mean is that every day experiences are discovered as new 'problems' and their 'cures' prescribed. For example, Melanie and Tim became exasperated with their mother's search for an understanding to her panic attacks as she feared that they might be affected by them. As Melanie said, 'look after yourself and get on with life. Every magazine you pick up is full of panic attacks and how to cure them. People will come up with a cure for breathing soon and then you'll be looking for an explanation for breathing attacks. You'll be saying "Oh dear, why am I breathing? What can be done about it?"' By 'getting on with life' and ceasing to understand her problem, Melanie's mum lost her panic attacks. Milner (2001) discusses how seeking to answer the 'why?' question supports dominant narratives and how it is not surprising that clients often believe the answer would be useful. However, when they are asked which would be better for them, to know 'why?' or to find a solution, they usually opt for the latter.

3   This disinterest in the cause of problems is replaced by an intense interest in competencies away from the problem. These can be specific, as in the case of Robin mentioned above, but sometimes it involves asking the client to tell you something good about themselves or running through a checklist of successful functioning to ascertain all the areas of living which have not been affected by the problem (for examples of recovery charts, see Appendix 3). Competencies can be highlighted by asking, 'did you know this about yourself?', a question which often surprises but invariably delights clients. The idea is that what is okay about a person can be utilised to fix what is not okay.

4   There is no focus on history or preoccupation with past events (other than successes) as the counsellor concentrates on what the client wants, or wants to change. Ruth, for example, responded very well to this as she had found her previous experience of problem-focused counselling (where she was encouraged to talk about her sexual abuse in order to express her feelings), absolutely exhausting and debilitating. Each session had left her so emotionally wrought that even her present low level of functioning was impaired. She

preferred to talk about how she could cope better in the present so that she could then feel well enough to face her past experiences. A further check that the client is setting the agenda for the conversation, not the counsellor who might be experienced in steering conversations on topics she thinks will be most fruitful, is by establishing a 'pass' convention early on for questions the client does not want to answer. Most clients respect the counsellor's authority so it is important to check the client's ability to say 'pass' early on.

5   Although emotions are not ignored, they are not the main focus of the conversation. How clients *do* emotions is considered much more productive. For example, Eva talked a great deal about her misery and inability to beat 'this disease' – her depression and self-harming. Asking her what she would be doing differently when she was happy yielded no useful information but she was able to say what she was doing differently when she was less unhappy: keeping busy, not drinking, planning her future, etc., all of which she was then able to do more.

6   Perhaps the most marked characteristic of solution talk is that it has no interest whatsoever in diagnosis, categorisation, pathologising or mending deficits. Instead, there is a search for difference, identifying uniqueness, and broadening competencies. For example, Samantha's referral form 'diagnosed' her 'voices' and violent behaviour as incipient schizophrenia, probably inherited from her mentally-ill mother. Rather than checking out whether her 'voices' were actual auditory hallucinations, or pathologising her violence as a response to the injunctions of the 'voices', she was asked more about the conversations she had with the voices. Although she heard the 'voices', she argued with them: 'I was grounded to my bedroom and I wanted a cig. This voice was saying, "go on, run off and get one". I went to the window and it said, "jump. Go on, jump". I said, "but I'll break my leg". "Go on. Do it, do it". It went on for ages. People think I'm mad, you know. I think I must be, it was a real voice.' From this conversation it was possible to identify Samantha's unique ability to stand up to the voice, which was not acting in her best interests.

Clients are often puzzled at the counsellor's interest in what is going well in their lives, especially where this involves identifying competencies well away from the problem, but this can be explained by using a medical metaphor with which they will be familiar. Here the contrast between different approaches to medicine is useful in that you can ask them which they would prefer: root and branch surgery on the problem or a boost to their immune system so that their mind and body can deal with the problem painlessly?

7   Neither is insight nor inference particularly prized; we find it so often to be wrong. Instead, respectful uncertainty is central. For example, Carl was talking about being good at sport when he was at school: 'Like an American jock, if you know what I mean.' The counsellor had an insight that he had enjoyed being a dominant male at school and perhaps found it more difficult when he became a junior male at work; possibly leading to his current extremely violent behaviour. She checked this out with him, only to find out that she was completely wrong: 'No. It kept me well in check, no energy to do owt else. I weren't interested in women, just sport. And it made no difference with the lads. We were all on a level at school. The head master, he used to deal with us if there was any arguments and he encouraged team work'. He went on to take complete responsibility for his violent attacks on other people: 'I can't blame anyone else. If I can't find a fight, then I'll create one, drunk or sober'. We do not ascribe clients' rejection of our insights to denial, rather we seek to understand them better by asking them to explain themselves to us.

8   Abandoning notions of denial also removes the problem of resistance. We simply search for clients' unique ways of cooperating with us. Resistance and interpretation have some meaning in the way we work but this is rather different from problem-focused counselling. More simply we see this as the client resisting the invitations of the problem to affect their lives adversely and any interpretations are those the client makes. This means that the counsellor is in less danger of storying a client outside the consulting room. This negative storying happens a great deal, we find, when we overhear conversations about clients on the telephone. It is so much simpler to ask the client.

9   Our way of working has no use for blame as a concept; this only leads to stultifying guilt. We find that boys whose behaviour attracts a good deal of censure are more likely to engage in counselling if they are invited to examine how they can do 'being good' rather than examining where 'badness' comes from. It is much more fruitful to look at behaviour in terms of responsibility-taking. This can involve inviting people to take more responsibility for

their *future* behaviour, mostly men or teenagers; or questioning whether the responsibility they are taking is reasonable, mostly wives, mothers, and children with troubled parents. The key issue here is people can only be responsible for their own behaviour.

Finally, this change of emphasis means that the counsellor is not the expert in problems – either the definition of them or the solutions. This is not to say that the counsellor is not influential in the questions asked, but she honours both professional and local knowledge. The latter, what the client tells you they know about the problem and their preferred solutions, is usually much more productive. We also consult the client as expert when we need help with other clients. We have discovered that there is no such thing as a typical or ordinary person; there are many people with previously untapped abilities, courage and tenacity. Identifying these qualities is of vital importance for successful counselling.

Before explaining how to get started on solution talk, in the next chapter we address the constructionist philosophy and principles of the approach as well as related values. Many of the values of problem-focused counselling still apply, and there are some similarities with cognitive-behavioural and person-centred counselling. Social constructionist thinking, however, adds some interesting dimensions to the more traditional values and ethics of counselling.

2

Practice principles

Counselling narratives

The principles and ethics of narrative and solution-focused brief counselling are closely tied in with the social constructionist and post-structural philosophy of the approach. We first simplify and briefly outline this philosophy; then we contrast this approach to the well-known work of Rogers, which superficially resembles our approach but is actually quite different. This will take us to the very purpose of counselling, the type of relationship it involves and, finally, to the values that govern it. If the reader finds the first half of this chapter difficult, we request you to be patient with it as it underpins what follows later.

Until about the 1960s, objectivist and structuralist explanations of the nature of people held sway. The central notion of objectivism – that knowledge is true if it corresponds with something objectively knowable and testable – and structuralism – that everything has a hidden inner structure capable of being discovered – was considered to be 'hard' scientific knowledge. This was viewed as more reliable and, therefore, superior to 'soft' knowledge or the wisdom of folk tales. Professional bodies acquired 'hard' knowledge that supported their expertness, their ability to perceive the inner structure of things, to diagnose and explain problems. White (1995: 45) argues that without structuralism, 'the psychopathologies and disorders could not have been invented', and that traditional psychotherapies play a significant role in the reproduction of dominant narratives.

By the 1970s this was being challenged by a cognitive revolution, particularly in the human sciences. 'Mind' itself was being redefined and seen as part of knowledge. This knowledge came to be understood not as something discovered by thought processes but as something *created* by them. 'Mind' became defined as a transactional entity, constructed by the very words used in talking with, and listening to, others.

By the 1980s psychotherapy was beginning to be influenced by this idea, as in some feminist literature; one of the most notable examples being Gilligan's (1982) work on moral development. History was seen as created by the writer and not just a record of real events. Family therapists, too, shifted from seeing themselves as objective observers of family systems to participants in them, co-creating meanings and helping to co-create new ones. This shift became known as *constructivism*, although this term is now generally more associated with the work of people like Maturana (1988) and Neimeyer (1993); being concerned primarily with *the processes* by which *individual* minds determine reality, rather than emphasising the *social* aspect. *Constructionism*, on the other hand, derives from the social construction of life in conversations, narratives and discourses; that is, linguistically, whether spoken, written or filmed.

It gradually became clear that the creation of meaning involves the *social* creation of new realities in a way that includes the cultural influences of any given time, along with their biases (see, for example, Walters, 1988). Gender, race and professional biases were increasingly exposed and the influence of power, poverty and interpersonal abuse began to be taken more into account (see, for example, Katz, 1996). By the late 1980s and early 1990s problems began to be seen as not just personal constructions but as social constructions (White and Epston, 1990). This *social constructionism* brought the realisation that even 'mind' was a product of constructionism – it was no longer private and personal but 'interdependent with culturally mediated realities' (Coale, 1998: 42). Social constructionism is consensual meaning construction through language, thus language comes centrestage and people are seen as being disempowered by dominant narratives. Payne (2000: 58) defines discourse as not just conversation but as a philosophical term meaning 'habitual ways of thinking and assuming, as a result of language habits, which are common currency within a particular social grouping', citing the differing narratives of football fans, the gay community, the medical or legal professions, and individual families as examples. These wider narratives have considerable power to determine how people's lives should be lived and have, therefore, potential to cause harm to those whose ways of living differ from the dictates of dominant narratives. This harm includes disempowerment and oppression, leading to feelings of guilt and shame; both of which undermine a sense of personhood (McLeod, 1997: 96), or the attribution of problems to personal character faults or pathologies.

Seeing such matters as constructed, rather than *de facto* or real, makes it is easier to question them; and question whether it is possible to 'know' in human science in the way we know in the physical sciences. After all, if problems are storied in narratives they are not real in the traditional sense, or at least we can be uncertain about them. In the social sciences the objectivist and structuralist stances have been laid open to question by the narrative stance. Thus many 'realities' are the result of lengthy and complex processes of construction and negotiated meanings that are embedded in time and culture (see, for example, Bruner, 1990); and searching for 'facts' is unhelpful in that facts are no more than dead metaphors with no potential for generativity (Rorty, cited in White, 1995). White writes that 'we are interpreting beings – active in the interpretation of our experiences as we live our lives, [but we need] a frame of intelligibility that provides a context for our experience and makes the attribution of meaning possible' (White, 1995: 15). Thus while stories provide the frames that make it possible for us to interpret our experience, actively making meaning, we are embraced by the stories we have about life. However, we do not have to go about life mindlessly reproducing dominant stories. For people to be empowered, their own stories, their 'soft' 'local' knowledge, needs to be honoured in the same way as any professional story. No story holds more truth than another; although some stories are more, and some less, helpful for coping with life. For Coale (1998), a counsellor's main skill has become that of a facilitator of helpful conversations, taking turns to create new and helpful narratives, and co-creating new possibilities for change in which the focus is switched from the past to the future.

Language gives meaning to events. Bertrand Russell is said to have commented that it is not the experience that happens to us, it's what we do to, or make of, that experience that happens to us. We make meaning out of our experiences by using words with which we are familiar, even though they may be inadequate to the task, there being no single story of life which is free of ambiguity and contradiction (White, 1995). In our work as counsellors this is particularly evident as we are dealing with stories most likely to hold multiple interpretations for all those involved: stories about strongly experienced emotions in interpersonal relationships. Coale (1998: 46) uses the word 'love' to illustrate this point. The Italian language uses two words to the English one: one meaning 'I want you', and the other, 'I care and am concerned for your welfare'. Even the latter is open to multiple meanings; for example, 'love' for a child can be that shown by a visiting parent during periodic contact, or that which a parent shows routinely in the daily care of a child, or that which drives a parent to seek residence with a child, or that which is shown when a parent gives up such a struggle. Similarly, language use has been found to be a major factor in African Caribbean educational disadvantage; these pupils and their white teachers erroneously assuming that they understood each other's language (Gibson and Barrow, 1986). A basic requirement in solution talk is careful thoughtfulness over the possible need to define what we talk about for the helpful reconstruction of situations and a nosiness about the precise meanings of other people's language.

In problem-focused counselling, the basic objectivist assumption is that words have stable meanings that match the meanings of realities and represent them as they actually are. While this stands up reasonably well for physical objects, such as a table, it fails for the inner world of experiences and feelings and for the interactional world of the social and the political. These worlds are mainly linguistically constructed: 'Words are the world' (White, 1995: 30). Indeed, language itself is constructed by its users and is culturally mediated. Language creates expectations, causes, dreams, history and culture itself. We use it to construct the meanings by which lives are lived and storied; it makes the very narratives of self and of world, each culture constraining its members by 'linguistically shaping' what people believe to be good, true and useful at a particular point in time (Coale, 1998: 48). People's experiences are organised by categories created by language. Take the word 'family', for example; many present-day families are far removed from what 'families' used to represent, or what powerful narratives define as desirable family forms.

This is a public use of language which powerfully defines and constrains experience, but there is also the private use of language, what Spacks (1986) refers to as the 'serious gossip' which has the capacity to undermine public language: 'Gossip as a phenomenon raises questions about boundaries, authority, distance, the nature of knowledge; it demands answers quite at odds with what we assume as our culture's dominant values' (Spacks, 1986: 12). Because social constructionism is antirealist, rather than separate fact from story we seek to deconstruct the perceptions from which the 'facts' are created and question the interests served by these perspectives. In conversation or in gossip others' realities can be questioned or undermined and oppressed people can construct victory, coping, survival or defeat, depending on how, in interaction with others, words are chosen to talk about a situation.

But because language has a built-in polarity whereby one word usually implies the absence of the opposite, for example normal = not abnormal, it can be used oppressively by denigrating the non-prototypical. Additionally, as language is literally man-made (Spender, 1985), less-powerful groups, such as women, may be denied words that apply only to the powerful group; for example, there is no female equivalent of captain and we say 'women doctors'. Graddol and Swann (1989) also refer to lexical gaps, there being no female equivalent for 'virility', nor any male equivalent of 'promiscuous'; and 'master' has a very different meaning from 'mistress'. From a very early age children learn from the responses of others the difference that words make and how the story they tell about what they do makes a difference.

Foucault (1972) discusses ways by which functions of social control can change from 'the person as monitor' to 'discourse as monitor', defining good, bad, moral to ensure compliance with norms. We each carry a social discourse in our heads and, therefore, we have an internal controller and we risk being diagnosed as mad or bad if what we say is not part of the dominant narrative. For example, people who are struggling to make sense of individual life experiences which do not 'fit' with their social narratives may experience this process as hearing voices which denigrate and undermine them. This is disturbing enough for a person but, should that person tell others about the 'voices', they are then likely to be entered into a psychiatric story. Rather than help them make sense of puzzling and contradictory experience, this further undermines their sense of personhood. Our institutions are mostly concerned with defending traditional beliefs and dominant narratives, rather than listening to the non-dominant. Diagnosis, 'the power to name' (Coale, 1998: 55), is an example of the power of language to label people – to call behaviour pathological. Feminist protest has been striving to revise this, add an interpersonal dimension to what is an individualistic culture, and introduce constructionist ideas in ways that open up new possibilities of meaning and action rather than label and categorise: 'If stories are fluid and changeable according to relation and context, then selves can change as narratives and the actions that emanate from them change' (Coale, 1998: 71).

Beliefs about 'the stable self' impede the process of exploring new possibilities and, if we impose such notions of self, we cannot help people to create alternative selves that are empowering. Likewise if we see some behaviours as having internal characteristics, they will also be seen as a stable part of self. Conflating a person with a problem serves to separate that person from others and lowers that person's individual responsibility for the behaviour. This is especially true where the behaviour is labelled as compulsive. Constructionism seeks to undermine this stance and to look at external narratives that the person has embraced. It also challenges all stage theories; their tendency to make male development the norm, and their tendency to create professional mystique and privilege. All professional beliefs are socially constructed and whether it is useful to present them as true depends on circumstances and whether they open up or close down possibilities and potential.

Foucault (1984) maintained that Western society has steadily built up ways of maintaining positions of power by the use of well-guarded expertise that perpetuates class divisions and influences morality and the law. The process involves persuading people, from a stance of benevolence, to internalise and maintain their own subordinate positions and identities and invites them to police each other in this regard (for a fuller discussion, see Ingleby, 1984). Counselling can involve helping a person to end the domination of these 'practices of power' that, for example, can lead to feelings of guilt at not performing oppressive duties or can involve continuing to live in fear of violence; it not being our uncommon experience that young women often seek counselling in order to help them learn how to manage their partner's violent behaviour. By challenging the metaphors of 'deep structures' or given 'natures', narrative ideas convey the thought that although the stories we tell ourselves and others are the most powerful influence in the way we live, they are also capable of being re-storied in a million ways that enlarge the sense of possibilities in our lives. This philosophy has clear implications for the aim of counselling.

Counselling aims

The identification, validation and strengthening of clients' inner resources is suggested as a basic aim of our work, which immediately begins to feel different from the unearthing of underlying conflicts. For the sake of clarity in this section, we will contrast narrative and solution-focused practice with the work of Rogers (1951, 1961). Rogers believed in the primacy of the person and that oppression should be overturned. He believed in the inner potential of people to deal with their lives, and that each person was to be respected as a person of worth, but he was still a structuralist who believed in helping people find their true authentic selves – who they really are. For social constructionists, our selves are socially built up and, while they should be free from oppression, they cannot be 'known' in that way. Rather than find our true selves, we seek to create who we want to be, which can include being different from what we have been. Self is not an innate essence with a 'real identity', so we help to free people from the 'real'; avoiding the tyranny of the 'authentic' and help to make it possible for clients to default on it. Neither do we engage in what White (1995) called the dominant 'feeling' narrative and the 'gymnastics' of the personal growth discourse which can, in themselves, be oppressive. For example, the commonly asserted aim of counselling to help people 'get in touch' with their feelings presumes not only that there is a desirable way of 'being' emotionally but that there is one way of achieving it – coming to terms with what has happened before a person can move on. Many people find it oppressive to have their refusal to rip off their carefully applied emotional bandages labelled as 'disassociation'. They frequently do *not* feel better for talking about emotionally fraught experiences, which seems to them to be another abusive experience. It is also our experience that when people ask to change their counsellor, their ability to make decisions and sensible choices is undermined when this is storied as 'resistance' to the counselling process. And how can anyone construct another person as 'needing 10 sessions'? Brief counselling aims instead to help people to refuse development towards an ideal imposed by social and cultural influences. For us there is no privileged viewpoint. This is not to say that all realities are relative; realities do exist *but* 'people's processes of knowing construct the versions of reality they come to experience and these are all we can hope to go by' (Winslade and Monk, 2000: 124). People talk many problems into existence so we need to look at the meanings created by people's narratives.

In the humanist tradition, Rogers saw the self as a self-contained individual unit. There followed a determination to find the true nature of the individual; objectivist thought suggesting that these natures were hidden by the process of unconscious repression which prevents growth and self-actualisation, frustrating authentic desires and needs. For Rogers, and many problem-focused counsellors, the emancipation of the individual from repression was the main aim. Needs were definable and capable of being met. We see this as an oppressive goal and needs' analyses as culturally determined (see, for example, Maslow, 1954), based on an individual self-determination that overrides social ethics and that sets up difficult standards of perfection, closing down questions of current experience and how our lives are lived. This leads to pressure to reproduce specified lives, ignoring people's own contributions to 'shaping' their lives. Constructionist workers do not go along with this encouraging of people to fit into defined concepts nor seek personal growth towards any ideal of selfhood. Expert knowledge that defines needs, selfhood, self-esteem and stages of development closes down and constrains options, and makes ethical choices more difficult. These ideas lead counsellors to perceive deficit and assumed inadequacies. Additionally if meeting needs and attaining self-esteem and actualisation were the aim it would raise the question of when could counselling end or when personal development should end, recruiting the counsellor into an impossible mission?

Payne (2000) puts forward the suggestion that, rather than personal development, the aim ought to be the *enrichment* of life, whereby we are responsible for developing new ways

> to enrich life with joyful activities while trying to bear in mind [our] access to such enrichment reflects a life of privilege and luxury compared with most people's lives on the planet. This is quite different from assuming that clients have deficiencies in personal development [needing] lengthy examination . . . to root out assumed sources of pain. (Payne, 2000: 208)

or that people need to grow or 'mature' by talking to us. Similarly Dolan (1998) considers that 'rooting out' assumed causes of pain focuses the person on their victimhood or, at best, their immediate survival. Moving from people's unsatisfactory pasts, where there are 'facts' we cannot change, to their preferred futures enables them to contemplate a life of joy. This may or may not involve re-storying aspects of the past or the present, though it usually involves talk about how people 'do' exceptions and what is the next small step.

Ethical implications

Usually people ask for help with a stuck problem, a perceived failure or a weakness. We can ethically assist them in meeting their preferred goals by avoiding assumptions of deficit, promoting various possibilities for developing their solutions, and co-authoring a new story of competence. While Rogers rejected the expert role for counsellors, in his view the counsellor was still the hero who liberated the client; the person whose relationship with the client was *central* to the process of growth. Part of the aim of Rogerian counselling was to build that 'healthy' relationship. In problem-focused counselling, too, 'relational depth' is sought in the belief that in a safe place, and in due time, the client will find a solution (see, for example, Mearns, 1994). Payne (2000) argues that this marginalises people's own relationships. We agree that our role is more ethical and effective when it facilitates 'real life' relationships. In other words the relationship with the counsellor should *not* be central. We aim to relate with warmth and empathy but *therapeutic* relationships need to be with the people who are important to clients and who join with them against the problem. We do not attempt to create a Rogerian-type therapeutic relationship on the grounds that this disempowers, lacks tranparency and is not genuinely two-way. We consider that the person consulting the counsellor should have charge of the agenda, any analysis should be shared openly rather than kept in the counsellor's head as a hypothesis, and that both parties should benefit from having their understandings and experience of people expanded.

We deliberately resist hypothesising about the (possibly) deep-seated nature of problems, remaining on the surface of what people say they want to do or change; being curious about people's strengths, the solutions implicit in exceptions to the problem and how these could be repeated. This involves avoiding developing hypotheses based on 'expert' theories, allowing more scope for the understanding of 'local' knowledge. It necessitates a careful use of language for the construction of greater and new competencies; for example, when things were better, asking how the person did this. Rather than seeking explanations which may cause us to advise, or listen to our own theories more than to the client, we accept that people are doing what they do and 'that this doing is the it that does it' (Cecchin, 1987: 408). Constructive talking about 'it' strengthens it: 'Solution focused therapists' main responsibility . . . is to help clients literally talk themselves out of their troubles by encouraging them to describe their lives in new ways' (Miller, 1997: 6).

A revision of values

Respect

Traditionally this has been seen as the fundamental value from which all other values and beliefs which ought to characterise a counsellor's attitudes flow. On respect, Egan says, 'The way you act will tell them a great deal about your attitude' (1998: 45). A respectful attitude includes caring for clients' welfare, seeing everyone as unique and viewing people as capable of choice. Respectful behaviour includes seeking to be competent, paying close attention to what people say, avoiding criticism or being judgmental, communicating empathy, expressing reasonable warmth, building on people's own resources, encouraging, supporting and challenging. Egan goes on to link respect with *genuineness*, by which he means avoiding stereotyped counsellor behaviour, keeping professional distance and boundaries by being spontaneous but 'not uncontrolled', being consistent with values, words and actions, and being willing to share personal experiences if this is helpful for the client.

Rogers considered the essential components of effective work to be a warm therapeutic relationship, acceptance, congruence and accurate empathy. While we can accept the helpfulness of these qualities of the relationship, we hold that we also should show respect for clients' goals (so long as they are legal and moral), for their religious beliefs and cultural differences, and take at face value what they say. Manthei (1997) adds that an anti-oppression stance and an understanding of the sources of injustice, disadvantage and prejudice is needed. This means we cannot ignore power issues, including our own power, but recognise that power has the potential to be productive as well as oppressive. Respect for clients involves limiting our purpose to the promotion of the client's own ideas about their best interests by suppressing any wish to help that is stronger than the client's or that includes our own goals.

Winslade and Monk (2000) claim that this ethic is also expressed in a reflexive stance and in curiosity about people's meanings. They base their position on a post-structural analysis of social relations, particularly of power. For example they do not take for granted subjectivity or being a moral agent in one's own life because 'lives are circumscribed by many discursive practices that limit opportunities

[and] operate against the possibility of taking a subjective position' (2000: 130). Thus respect in our combined approach requires:

• Listening to how narratives operate in people's lives and listening to their wishes to oppose these influences.
• Looking for opportunities to give people their own voice.
• Listening to that voice without being confused by the problem. The problems are the problem; not the people. We need to be especially careful not to let the problem story represent the totality of the person.
• Refusing to 'sum people up', remaining uncertain, open to contradictions, and to possibilities beyond the known.
• Speaking to people as agents in the creation of their lives, their worlds, and their selves.
• Legitimating people's wishes to be subjects and producers of narratives rather than objects of their operation.
• Avoiding assumptions that might limit people's potential for self-agency, such as ideas about deficit, pathology or any single label.
• Not remaining neutral on issues of subjugation, supporting people in their challenge of privilege (e.g. patriarchy) but expressing this support in ways that neither objectify nor pathologise the oppressor.

Confidentiality

Counsellors also show respect for confidences by explaining the limits of confidentiality where there are legal and/or safety issues. We would add that this includes respecting people's wishes about contact with other professionals; particularly not hypothesising about them over the telephone with the people who refer them for counselling in the first place. We link confidentiality with transparency; that is, by not operating in a manner that is not understood and ensuring that people know where they stand with us. An important part of transparency is the co-authorship of records. This involves not just open access to files but actually taking care at the first session to ensure that the client sees, and can comment on, any referral details supplied by others; and subsequently posting a copy of the file record to each client. Open recording is used with written feedback to people which they often share with others. The approach also includes explaining the process of supervision to them and, particularly in the case of young people, writing PRIVATE AND CONFIDENTIAL on any letter and records posted to the address of their choice.

Because the work involves talking much more about competencies and possibilities than deficits and problems, many issues of confidentiality that trouble problem-focused counsellors do not exist in solution talk. We are confident that our co-authored records could be subpoenaed, for example, without our worrying that these would portray damaging information. Also we have found that when people complete solution talk they frequently are happy to have their success celebrated in public, to receive 'certificates' and cut celebratory cakes. In talking of competence, possibility and exceptions to the problem more that the problem itself, publicity replaces some of the older confidentiality.

Self-determination

For Egan (1998), this is a guiding value which he describes as self-responsibility. It means clients taking an active part in tackling problems, whether they be of their own making or not. It means encouraging people to take the lead in problem management; persisting in doing so, and making links between behaviours and their results; thus raising their expectations of being able to do this. This he suggests is furthered by increasing counsellors' expertness and attractiveness so that they are more influential in getting people to manage their lives more effectively. Although traditional workers taking this 'expert' stance were reminded to allow people choices, there remained a caveat that the task might include encouraging and influencing them to do what the counsellor considered necessary for change. Thus self-determination was often limited by the counsellor's perception of clients' abilities to reason or make good choices, an added danger being the increase of people's powerlessness. To address this Egan suggests that counsellors see themselves as hired servants who help others to be more effective at living, but the responsibility for running the business remains with those who hire the worker, who is a mere passing support system.

In solution talk, because the work involves finding exceptions and empowering people to repeat them and develop new possibilities for being, the issue of self-determination is more easily accommodated. The counsellor's stance is one of uncertainty, since we distrust scientific 'knowing', and we respect people's self-agency by holding them accountable for their own actions, but without judging or blaming. Of course we acknowledge that we can have inner tyrants that push us towards imposing certain values onto others, for example in relationships between the sexes. One way we provide a check against this is by adopting what Tamasese and Waldegrave (1996) call 'just therapy', consulting colleagues who are more similar to clients than ourselves. Elliot (1997) adds that the counsellor can create space for evaluation of the session by the client, have people who are experienced in the problem as consultants, and refer the client back to others in her community for comments on the work.

Since goals are negotiated rather than imposed and we remind people of their right to 'pass' on any questions asked, since we do not strive to liberate people from their repressions or to place ourselves central in the helping project, our tendency to unduly influence could be less than in problem-solving counselling. Solutions are co-constructed with clients so that the solutions are their own. Tasks are suggested and are carried out only if the client wishes; if they come up with a better idea they are invited to do that instead. Showing optimism and confidence in people's abilities helps to promote self-determination. The expertness of the counsellor is restrained by respect for the client's knowledge and potential and by honouring their right to choose; concentrating on asking questions that help people to take more control of their lives and resist disempowering narratives.

Dealing with resistance

Partnership is the name of the game – focusing on the cooperation of the counsellor with the client rather than the co-operation of the client with the counsellor. It is the client who defines the problem, the goal and what would be a satisfactory outcome, so that any so-called resistance towards the counsellor is seen as the client telling us how they want us to cooperate with them. Our job is to locate the seeds of solutions in the client's current behaviours and to open up possibilities for them. 'Resistance' has more to do with the puzzlement of the counsellor then with the obduracy of the client. It is counsellor error: 'There are no resistant clients, only inflexible therapists' (Bandler and Grinder, 1979). De Shazer (1991) holds that there is no such thing as resistance, only different ways of cooperating and it is for counsellors to work in ways that fit clients' views. When people seem to not cooperate they are telling us how they think change happens, what Iveson (1990) refers to as shouting louder to make themselves understood. We need to understand their views and cooperate with *them*; they are letting us know how not to help (Parton and O'Byrne, 2000). By working with clients, rather than against them, cooperation becomes inevitable.

Individualisation within cultures

Traditionally, this has involved treating each person as different from everyone else, but the holding of hypotheses about problems and diagnoses necessarily categorised and labelled clients, undermining individualisation. The constructionist approach is essentially individualised and particular care is taken to respect religious and cultural backgrounds. Difference is positively respected with the onus on the counsellor to bridge the cultural gap, using the term culture in the widest sense. There is a cross-cultural element to most of our work and this involves differences of language, folklore, religion, art and customs as well as differences of age, gender, race and socio-economic grouping. We are wary of overemphasising the similarities of human experience; when recognising similarities we must also recognise uniqueness. It helps to know one's own culture, with its biases and stereotypes, and ask ourselves if every client would say we were sensitive to their culture. Above all, we seek out their reality in detail, their rating of the problem and its difficulty, and especially utilising everything they bring to the session in terms of exceptions, unique qualities, even so-called problems. More simply, we would recommend that individualisation is best achieved by saying to the client that you don't fully understand their world, so will they please explain it to you.

Safety

Protecting the safety of clients from violence and other harm is a prime concern. This applies also to working with couples, particularly where one is violent, and children; not only our dealing with them but by reporting any dangerous situation to the appropriate authorities. Our own safety, too, can be an issue and we are expected to take reasonable precautions and avoid undue risks to ourselves or our colleagues.

Safety for clients involves their feeling safe with us, and our being aware of the implications of touch and being gender sensitive concerning closeness/personal space. Manthei (1997) says there must be no touch except where it can clearly be said how it will serve the client's needs. Touch has many meanings and we cannot assume what the client's meanings are, let alone our own intentions. We support fully the BACP code on safety; agencies and individual counsellors need to set out their policies and procedures for ensuring that safety is addressed.

Empathy

For Rogers, communicating accurate empathy is a core condition for effective counselling. This often meant trying to second-guess how difficult or painful a situation was for the client and reflecting that verbally; for example, by saying something like 'this must be really difficult for you'. Empathy involves trying to understand the experience as a client understands or experiences it, getting a feeling for being in it with the client. Basic empathy – listening genuinely and respectfully – is compared with advanced empathy whereby the counsellor goes beyond the client's experience and sees meanings that she cannot see fully as yet. Egan gives the example of a person saying they are angry and the counsellor also sensing hurt. This involves listening with 'a third ear' to what is implicit or only half said, but it is really only guessing and risks alienating the client. Egan says it is listening for understanding rather than for evaluation. It requires accurate listening, not pretending to understand, not parroting what is said, but rather setting aside biases, being gentle and reasonably tentative, noting the client's reactions. Above all empathy is said to get close to feelings, to being supportive, yet challenging – it is seen as essential for an effective relationship between counsellor and client.

Research suggests that it is the quality of that relationship that ultimately affects outcome (see, for example, Gurman, 1977; Miller, Duncan and Hubble, 1997). This is important to the constructionist approach to helping too, although we would define it more as *the client feeling understood*, rather than a function of the counsellor. Following Turnell and Lipchik (1999), we move away from *understanding* people's emotional experiences, seeing emotion, cognition and behaviour as interdependent, and focusing more on *engaging at an emotional level*. This involves validating any feelings that are expressed and responding, verbally and non-verbally, to a client's communications, going at their pace, listening to their words rather than to one's own theories or interpretations, and showing interest. Active listening requires genuine interest and a belief that there is no such thing as an ordinary person.

More significant than developing empathic abilities is focusing on what the client wants, on their (frequently only partly developed) goals and aspirations. Understanding what a person *wants* will usually lead to their feeling understood. In solution-focused work the use of scaled questions refines this further, as does the search for exceptions and the future miracle question (these techniques are explained in Chapter 3). Likewise, past successes can be related to what is now wanted. When this is done well and included in the summing up or in a letter, feeling understood is further strengthened and a greater mutual understanding of the situation is developed for both counsellor and client, without much emphasis on emotions as such, although these are accepted and validated. People's complaints are talked about in the language in which they are described by the client, not translated into professional language where the words have less meaning for the client.

It is important to distinguish the helpful humanist notion of 'understanding', which means understanding clients' points of view and their goals, from the individualist notion of 'understanding' what is wrong with people, which involves explaining the causes of their problems. In our practice, the need to understand that causation is downplayed. We can never know exactly what another person means by what they say, we can only strive for 'creative misunderstanding'. De Shazer (1991: 69) goes further and argues that this helps to keep counsellors humble and reflective, checking misunderstandings with people and preparing us to co-construct a reality that is more satisfactory to the client. A simple way of doing this is by adding an afterthought to the notes posted to the client, in which second thoughts are expressed as possibilities to be evaluated by the client (Epston, 1998). As Turnell and Lipchick (1999) point out, it is the client's role to decide whether s/he is understood and it is the counsellor's role to build understanding of the client's *description and experience* of the problem, and their position on it. That is not to say, however, that we do not value traditional ways of building empathy as a basic condition of the encounter; simply that such empathy alone is not enough. Whilst it may help us to enter the client's experience to some extent, on its own it does not create space for thinking about how things can be different.

That requires a greater appreciation of curiosity than was previously the case.

Challenging

Egan (1998) discusses challenging as a key element in counselling; in particular challenging self-defeating and self-blaming stories. He says challenges should be delivered with care and respect, taking into account people's ability to handle them. He suggests the usefulness of pointing out successes when people feel they have failed in everything or pointing out resources they may have failed to use, the intention being to strengthen rather than weaken the client. He also invites people to challenge themselves. Rather than challenge, the constructionist approach *invites* clients to evaluate their stories of blame or non-accountability. This is more a process of subverting the stories by proffering different stories for the client to evaluate, although scaled and exception-finding questions could be said to act as a creative challenge to feelings of hopelessness. Additionally in narrative practice there is the challenge of examining the relationship between the person and the problem, how the problem affects their life, and how they affect its life; for example, by being welcoming towards it at some time. When this happens, they are invited to comment on how the advantages the problem brings them can be retained at the same time as a solution is found to that problem. We could say that these invitations are based on respect for the person's self-agency and self-responsibility; underlining clients' power to choose encourages personal responsibility-taking.

Self-challenging

Counsellors, too, need to be challenged and held accountable, at least by themselves. We would argue that in particular we are accountable for using constructive non-pathologising language, for not labelling, for not blaming but rather holding people accountable for the future, for recognising clients' knowledge, for opening up possibilities and for remaining uncertain. Certainty could well be unethical. A diagnostic label may be useful or it may be harmful, but in either case is not necessary for intervention and it risks creating a false certainty.

Consulting with a 'similar' supervisor aids this process, for example by spotting any tendency to use pathology language or to slip into hypothesising.

Personal qualities

Specific qualities in a counsellor are considered desirable, if not essential, for effective client relationships. Manthei (1997) places self-awareness high on his list. This includes a capacity for humble self-questioning, asking, 'what impact am I having, what skills need improving, what bias am I showing, am I optimistic?' One might add, 'is my own life satisfactory, am I using my work to address my need as well as the need of others?' Mental flexibility is also mentioned, as is the ability to be reflective and reflexive in practice. This is best checked out by evaluating each session with the client, asking if it has been helpful and what the counsellor would be doing differently if it had been more helpful. As discussed earlier, warmth towards others, non-conditional positive regard and acceptance are necessary in all forms of counselling. A non-dominant attitude, not wishing to control people, being open-minded and objective are also listed, as is maturity and tolerance of tension and ambiguity (Manthei, 1997: 44). It is difficult, however, to measure such qualities; objectivity is, as we have argued earlier, not really possible anyway. Dolan (1998) considers enthusiasm and a consistently held belief in the capacity of people to find their own solutions to be essential qualities. While a counsellor might do well to ponder on them and discuss them in supervision, in our view it is the client's perception of these qualities in a counsellor that matters most for effective understanding.

Helping relationships

Not every relationship with every client should be the same: 'The idea that one perfect kind of relationship or alliance fits all clients is a myth' (Egan, 1998: 42). One client may respond well to warmth, another may respond better to a businesslike relationship. Communicating a great deal of empathy might put off a person who fears intimacy, so even respect and genuineness need to be expressed in ways that respond to how clients are presenting themselves.

Different theoretical and philosophical orientations towards helping affect the sort of relationships we have with clients and, as has been indicated earlier, in narrative and solution-focused work we are less concerned that the relationship with the counsellor should be the (only) therapeutic one – relationships with significant others are seen as the primary therapeutic relationships. The focus is more on trying to figure out with people what they think they are doing, want to do and can do, establishing their story and then enriching it, thickening the plot with forgotten or unstoried abilities, achievements and successes.

The Rogerian notion of congruence, being aware of one's feelings and not concealing them from the client, is achieved in a constructionist approach through transparency: 'self-monitoring as regards our culturally and socially formed assumptions, beliefs and behaviours' (Payne, 2000: 216), and trying to avoid their worst effects by *sharing* them with people. In doing this we are addressing beliefs more than feelings, being open about any possible culture-gap so as to avoid inequality of power, undue influence or a central relationship in the client's life. We are not seeking to cure deficit but to help with the management of a problem, learning from the client what is useful to them. There is a commitment to empowerment through identifying and building the client's own solutions, however small, and opening up possibilities for doing more of that.

Summary

Social constructionism provides the theoretical underpinnings of a solution-focused approach to brief counselling. The philosophy includes an unwavering belief in clients' capacities to find their own solutions, thus the guiding principle is if it works, do more of it; if it doesn't work, do something different. As Berg and Reuss (1998) point out, solution-focused practice is simple but not simplistic; the techniques providing a discipline within which the counsellor can remain true to the philosophy and principle. Narrative approaches to brief counselling are influenced by social constructionism but there is also an emphasis on poststructuralism. This accommodates power issues in that the theory highlights the reality that while there are no 'truths', some 'truths' have more power than others. Thus the philosophy (the person is not the problem) and guiding principle (questioning unhelpful stories) means that the practice concentrates more on unique outcomes rather than the exception-finding of solution-focused counselling.

Marrying the two approaches in solution talk causes certain tensions. *Narrative* work is more about talking about problems, in particular their *influence*, and clients' heroic resistance to them; adding stories from other people sometimes. *Solution-focused* practice moves into *progressive* narrative sooner – it draws narrative from the miracle question, adding very little – certainly not specifying the new story. It virtually bypasses discussion of problems and spends more time talking about life when the problem is no more, when there is *solution*, seeing problems and solutions as only nominally related. The past however is not ignored:

> we talk of the past in a way that is focused on how they hope things will be *different*. It's not the retelling that leads to change but talk about how the re-telling will make a difference and what will be happening when they feel they have talked enough about the past so the talking can move forward somewhere. (Durrant, SFT e-mail list 2000)

The *values* of the combined approach are seen as something we *do*, that is transparent and measurable, not mere ideas in our heads. We consider we are being unethical when we fail to:

- empower our clients. If we don't empower we disempower;
- contribute in every conversation to the linguistic construction of a positive or heroic story, of potential and possibility, of belief in as yet unused resources, and belief in people's own as yet unknown knowledges;
- honour the obligations implicit in 'respect';
- question discrimination or oppression;
- take care to ensure that the words we use do not reduce possibilities;
- avoid becoming central in clients' lives;
- address safety issues.

3

Practice techniques

Solution talk routinely uses key techniques but does not do so in a routine way. The techniques evolved from a close study of what works and they fit with the philosophy and principles outlined in the previous chapter. They continue being developed in various creative ways by those practising brief counselling. We do not suggest that the techniques necessarily be used in the order set out in this chapter; indeed in most practice they are intertwined, mixed, repeated and varied according to the preference of the counsellor and their evaluation of what fits best with how the client is working. Before we begin we repeat that the approach has a non-pathological stance; that is, we assign no pathological significance to people's problems nor define them as deficits, maintaining a focus on preferred futures. The aim is to be practical and parsimonious, being aware of what one does *not* need to do. The solution-focused approach has particularly been described as minimalist in that it only does what is essential in drawing solutions from the client. When observed it looks easy and sounds simple but it is neither; requiring great discipline to *refrain* from doing what is unnecessary and from ideas of pathology.

Validation

Clients' emotions are not ignored; when there is a description of a distressing situation, a loss or a painful experience, the various emotions exhibited are accepted, acknowledged and validated. However, this validation and the implied empathy involved has a 'twist'. As O'Hanlon (1995) explains, the counsellor acknowledges the emotion but adds a word that implies a possibility of difference, that there is some hope of change. For example; if a client says, 'I feel suicidal', we would reply, 'that must be scary, have you been suicidal *before?*'

If the answer is affirmative, we would follow up with, 'how did you recover *last time?*' Similarly a statement such as, 'I can't beat this depression' would be responded to with, 'so you have not been able to beat it *so far*'. These little added words make a hole in a seemingly impossible difficulty, providing an opening for possible strengths or solutions. By way of further validation, O'Hanlon adds that clients need to hear that they can experience what they experience and it is okay, and that it is also okay not to feel as they do – and that they don't *have* to feel either. The door to possibilities needs to be opened just a tiny bit to avoid jumping into hope in a way that would leave the client behind. We find that going very slowly early on actually speeds up solution-finding.

Although problems are listened to carefully, we do not stay with them longer than is needed for the person to feel heard. If the client is beginning to repeat them, this may require a clear statement such as, 'so you have had a terrible time – it's amazing – in spite of it all you are still here'. This turns troubles into compliments, providing the beginning of a different conversation. An extended discussion of problems can be counterproductive; without identifying exceptions lengthy problem-saturated stories become self-fulfilling prophesies. Similarly we do not seek the cause of problems; seeing it as more important to focus on understanding the seeds of solutions that are usually in the story.

A history of possibilities

Rather than facilitating a detailed history of difficulty and failure or search for cause, our main interest in history is to search for the 'invitations' the person received, for the social influences linked to the language of patriarchy, sexism, racism or sense of entitlement. We ask questions about what methods were used to recruit the person into the problem, what seduction was whispered in their ear. We ask what sort of influence the problem has had on them, their family, their relationships and their pride in themselves. This is to develop a sense of alienation between them and the problem and a sense that it is worth while standing up to it or eliminating it. The relationship clients have with some problems is not always clear, so this questioning can be widened to include other significant persons, with questions like, 'what would your mother say makes her proud of you?' Thus we listen to history in a different way, searching for the *relationship* between client and problem; competencies or good qualities away from the problem; what the client wants to change; and what difference that will make in their lives. Where clients find it difficult to say anything positive about themselves, we encourage them by posing questions such as, 'if you were in an overloaded lifeboat, having to explain why you should not be ejected, what reasons would you give?' The narrative becomes 'progressive', implying movement towards a goal. It is not a fantasy narrative but one based on concrete details of exceptions to the problem or unique outcomes – however small.

Externalising

White (1990: 95) talks about how people come to believe that they are the problem and suggests separating the two via externalising conversations in which he asks about clients' unique outcomes to their problems. These unique outcomes are the occasions when the client stood up to the problem, was heroic in some way, delayed the problem or escaped from its influences. To encourage the client to have a different relationship with both the problem and the narrative which supports it, early on in the discussion the problem is spoken of as an external enemy oppressing the person. This aids the non-pathologising of the client; it is the *problem* that is the problem.

Externalising helps the client stand back from the problem and recover a sense of self-agency as ways of subverting it are discussed. Discovering the cunning ways of the problem helps clients to separate themselves from their own subjugation. It helps if the client can give the problem a name as soon as possible, but this is not always possible without some help. For example, a woman with serious relationship problems with her mother-in-law could only say of the problem, 'It's indefinable'. As the discussion moved on, it emerged that the problem had many branches and the counsellor said, 'like tentacles?' 'Yes, it's a giant octopus, gripping me in several ways'. From then on it was spoken of as 'the octopus' and the conversation was about which 'tentacle' to disarm first. Metaphors are a major part of naming and O'Hanlon (1995) has developed a set of metaphorical frames based on imprisonment, sport, war, seduction, crime and others. For example, 'how did the problem try to get you on the ropes? How did you loosen its grip, get out of the corner?' (For a fuller discussion, see Parton and O'Byrne, 2000.) Metaphors are not interpreted; instead a story is developed in which the client is active and in which the problem is in opposition to them rather than a pathology inside them.

Although it is important to use metaphors suggested by the client, we do try to avoid excessively masculine 'fighting' metaphors with males who have problems with temper control, adapting animal metaphors where appropriate. For example, Robin said of his father, 'he's like an elephant – he only moves to eat'. This was followed up with, 'do you need some elephant training skills?', but the reality that small children have limited power in the family (for a fuller discussion, see Freeman *et al.*, 1997) was acknowledged by adding a caution, 'what's the safest way to train an elephant without getting trampled upon?' We also use metaphors which relate to clients' literary preferences; Hagrid from the Harry Potter books is a regular favourite with young children and Jane Eyre is a symbol of resistance for many young women.

Externalisating conversations aid the development of alternative stories and encourage the client to take action against the problem. They emphasise context, deconstruct the objectification of people, and challenge the dominant narratives through which 'disorders' and 'pathologies' are constructed. Clients are helped to *experience* themselves as separate from their problems. Externalisations thus provide an 'exposé' of the techniques of the government of lives; by naming dominant forces, they invite people to take up a position towards the problem and consider whether they want to continue living with it. Externalisation opens the problem to subversion in which both client and counsellor are partners. In the case of violent or oppressive behaviour by the client, however, accountability is not to be minimised and so it is the beliefs and attitudes supporting the violence that are externalised, enabling other ways of responding to situations to be found.

Here are some more examples of externalising questions: 'when did Depression move in with you?,' 'What does it whisper in your ear?', 'What effect has Temper Tantrum had on your family?' This can lead to finding moments when things were better; for example, 'Tell me about when you made Temper Tantrum wait', or 'Tell me about a time when you did not fall for the lies Anorexia was telling you?', 'What does that say about how you can be in the future?'

Exceptions

Wittgenstein is famous for saying that the only interesting thing about a problem is that it carries within itself an idea of a solution. That idea is contained in an exception, occasions when the problem was less or not there, when life was free of it to some extent. This implies that the solution was present, even if only for a moment or partially. De Shazer (1991) maintains that there are always exceptions, otherwise how would a client know they had a problem? He defines an exception as, 'whatever is happening when the complaint is not' (1988: 52) (this is different from White's 'unique outcomes' which are standing up to the problem or resisting it). There is nothing that always happens in human relationships; no-one takes drugs every minute of the day or steals night and day or loses their temper with everyone, but if exceptions are not asked about they go unnoticed. Even if the client cannot identify an exception, exceptions can be pretended; for example, by living for a week *as if* the problem was less of a problem.

When exceptions are found we examine them in detail; asking questions such as, 'What was different?', 'What do they say about you?', and especially, 'How did you do that?' This latter question is most powerful in the development of self-agency and empowerment. It contains 'you' and 'do'. The more this 'doing' is talked about, the more the locus of control shifts to the client. This is an essential shift for those clients who are near to giving up and who feel their lives are controlled by others or by their 'natures' or moods. We often find that persistent offenders and looked-after children, those whose lives are largely controlled by teachers, police, peers and social workers, most frequently express this belief.

Exceptions create stories that make it possible to learn from what is already there and to see success. They can be amplified with questions such as, 'what have others noticed?, what difference does that make?, what will it be like when this is happening more? how do you do it?, who could help you to do it more?' Client competencies can be complimented and underlined; what works can be used more. Dolan (1991) describes working with exceptions as following the client's easiest path.

Solutions can happen without the problem being touched as they have only a 'nominal relationship' with the problem (de Shazer, 1993: 119), so exception-finding questions can relate to life just before the first appointment. It has been found that many exceptions happen between the appointment being made and being kept. These 'pre-session' changes are most useful as they are attributable solely to the client and not to the counsellor's work. The counsellor can ask, 'has any small change happened since you rang?' and 'how did you do that?' Solutions are constructed by putting 'any differences that are noticed to work in such a way as that difference opens up the possibility of new meanings, behaviours etc., developing' (de Shazer, 1993: 116). For example, the counsellor can ask, 'is any small part of your goal already happening sometimes?', 'are there times when the problem is less in some way?', 'when are your best moments?', 'what were you doing that was different then?'

Beginning brief counsellors can have difficulty with the 'how do you do that?' question if the client answers, 'I don't know'. Clients often say this as they are expecting you to supply the answers. To counter this apparent passivity, born of not realising what they know, we take the view that if they did it they must know how to do it, although they often do not *yet* know that they know this. Therefore we slow down and give them time. There are various options for responding to this situation; all of which shift the expertise from the counsellor to the client; you could try one or two of these:

- No reaction, other than a puzzled expression (after all it is now the client's turn to speak).
- Maybe you know and don't know at the same time – that's hard to say . . .
- Acknowledge they 'don't know' and wait, pretending that's not the answer.
- I always think that when people do things they must have some idea of how to do it . . .
- Of course you don't know yet; so what do you think?
- Okay, so what do you think your Mum/best pal would know?
- Suppose you did know, what might the answer be?
- Perhaps I have not asked the question in a helpful way – how could I ask it better?
- [for small children] Oh, I see. It's a secret. Okay.
- Perhaps you might like to study what happens next time and see if you can spot how you do it?

We sometimes repeat the first of these after any other option chosen. Sometimes we do not wonder 'how', but carry on as if the question had been answered. Experienced counsellors report that as they practice more they get fewer 'don't knows'. How we ask a question shows our underlying assumption of client expertise: 'When we expect people to know we seem to find ways to ask questions that give clients the space to do their own creative work' (Zeiglar, SFT e-mail list, 2000). We become better at timing questions and assume people *do* know, but perhaps it takes time for that belief to be so strong as to show through in our language (verbal and non-verbal). So, without pressing for a good answer, we are quietly confident that people know but just don't realise it yet. They may, however, be able to suggest a better way of asking such a difficult question.

Agreeing goals

The basic question for identifying a well-formed goal is, 'how will you know when you don't need to come for counselling any more?' De Shazer maintains that well-formed goals are one of the best predictors of success. A well-formed goal is about what the client wants (so long as it is moral and legal), but it helps if it is realistic, achievable, time-limited, consisting of the presence or start of something rather than the absence or end of something; for example, the start of dry beds rather than ending wet beds (which is impossible to say when it happens). Goals are of the future and talk of when they are achieved is itself a major intervention, creating more possibility of it happening. Picturing life without the problem and the effects on family and others helps create life without the problem. It not only generates optimism but moves the person forward from 'problem talk' to 'solution talk' without ever having to consider the process of getting there. For those for whom major change is impossible; for example, getting back a severed limb or a deceased family member or getting out of prison, the realistic goal is usually one of getting by with hope. We tend to avoid the term coping as it has negative and sexist connotations – women are often expected to cope or put up with, while men manage and succeed. With clients who have no faith in any change, we can talk about life when this pessimism is overcome; otherwise, what else do they want from counselling? We do not accept negative goals; for example, 'I will not be worrying constantly about food', leads only to a possibly terrifying void, so we ask, 'what will you be doing *instead*?': 'Change will not be sustained if a void is not filled with something new. Stories that only emphasise giving up troublesome behaviours actually direct clients' attention to that which they are supposed to avoid.' (Miller, 1997: 75). Just giving up something leaves no direction for the future as well as losing previous skills in getting by.

Some clients have great difficulty in expressing a clear goal; for example, Duggie said that he wasn't sure what he wanted: 'Like when me and the girlfriend fall out, I attack her. I don't think I'm going to attack her. I just do it. I don't like arguing . . . I want some advice, if you know what I mean'. We break down such vague goals into solvable elements by asking detailed behavioural questions such as, 'What will you be doing differently when you are not having arguments?' and 'can you tell me about a time when you stopped an argument from developing without attacking her?' We sometimes ask, 'if this were a shop where you could buy a solution to your problem what would you want to buy to-day?' If the reply is, 'I don't know', we may ask, 'how will your life be better/different when you do know?' They may say, 'I'd feel better', and we may say, 'great, so when you feel better what will you start doing that you don't do now?' The 'miracle question' is frequently used to aid goal development.

The miracle question

This name has been given by de Shazer (1988: 5) to a specific question that has been shown to work particularly well in goal development and 'future talk'. It is quite long and similar to a guided fantasy; it goes like this:

> Suppose that when you leave here you go out and do what you have to do, you get home, have something to eat and later on you go to bed [pause]. While you are asleep something miraculous [or magical] happens and the problems that brought you here vanish, in the click of a finger [pause]. But because you were asleep you don't know this has happened [pause]. When you wake up in the morning, what do you suppose will be the first thing you will notice that will tell you that this has happened?

(We would be cautious about associating words like miracle and magic with bedtime with a child who may have been sexually abused. 'Wonderful' works equally well.)

This question has certain key features. It is the start of a new story and the miracle is an ordinary miracle in that it is part of the ordinary things the client is going to do. It invites the person to step into 'solution talk' and to discuss the differences. It helps them to articulate the very first signs they will notice tomorrow and to build a 'video picture' of what will be going on, what else will they notice, what other people will notice that is different, what they and others will be saying and so on. This picture is extended with a repeated question, 'what else?', or in the instances where a client says they would have won the lottery, 'can any of this happen before the money arrives?'

Sometimes clients say the miracle would be that they would be re-united with lost loved ones, to which the reply might be, 'what advice would that person give you for handling the problem?' Or where schoolchildren say that their miracle would be that all their teachers have been sacked, 'how would *you* be behaving differently with the new teachers?' The solution begins to be constructed without discussing the problem in depth or its causes and without even considering how it can be overcome. The ensuing conversation opens up real possibilities for alternative ways of being. This question therefore disconnects the solution from the problem and, as other people's reactions are talked about, interactional descriptions are generated. Problem definition becomes unnecessary. Change is cast as something that just happens and the question suggests that the client must work at recognising it. Of course the 'miracle' will have a very different meaning for each client, which will only become evident as the conversation is continued, but the word can encourage and facilitate a progressive narrative.

Some counsellors simplify the miracle question to something like, 'When your problems have been solved what will you notice that is different?' Such shortened versions do not seem to work as well. Neither do crystal ball versions such as, 'suppose we could look into the future', although we have had successes with a 'back to the future' version which goes like this:

> You know the Michael J. Fox film *Back to the Future*, where the young man goes for a ride into the future, or the past, in the mad professor's car? Let's get into that car and fly to your house in the future. We park outside and creep up to the window, and you see yourself at [choose an age which is appropriate for each client's preferred future]. You can tell that this person has their life totally sorted out. What are they doing that tells you this?

(Get as much detail as possible about what they are doing, who is with them, what the room looks like, whose photographs are on the wall, etc.), then ask, suppose this person sees you peering through the window and invites you in; you ask them how they managed to do all this. What might they say? [then] where do they suggest you should start? [or] Have they a word of comfort for you in this time of trouble?

In this way clients are invited to talk to their competent self and they often discover solutions and ideas they did not know they had. A focus on solutions through these questions can show people the way forward. Being able to imagine a better future is an important asset. The described becomes possible because what is talked about is pictured and internally *experienced as* possible. Such conversations seem to help clients to begin talking themselves into changes. Where a client has no sense of a competent future, it is possible to reverse the miracle question and ask about a nightmare scenario instead (for a discussion of the latter, see Berg and Reuss, 1998).

Following the miracle question, we ask, 'is any small part of that miracle happening already?' If so this can be amplified with questions like, 'how do you do that?', 'is there anything else?', 'how is that different?', 'what do people say?', 'how can you do more of that?', 'how will your thinking be different?'

There is no way of predicting what use a client will make of these questions. As de Shazer has said (SFT e-mail, 2000), we don't even know what question we have asked until we hear the reply. One client who was so severely depressed that he could see no possibility of change, said at the next session, 'I have solved the miracle thing; I've called it the Cursed Miracle; I am cursed for life with depression and somehow I make the best of it'. It is important not to rush or force the issue; for many people 'getting by' is their preferred solution, especially where their relationships are very complicated and they do not aspire to ideal solutions, which they view as self-centredness. De Shazer points out that the miracle question is more like a strategy that involves many 'techniques', so we seek to ask it as if it were never asked before. We may be very familiar with the question but we can never be familiar with the responses, so we always have a genuine curiosity which is conveyed to the client:

Scaled questions

Having asked the miracle question and explored the reply, de Shazer likes to follow with a scaled question such as: 'suppose we had a scale from 0 to 10, and 0 was how things were when you first contacted us and 10 was the day after the miracle, how near to 10 are you to-day?' These questions were developed by solution-focused thinkers to help clients express in a precise way what might otherwise be difficult to articulate. For example, 'suppose we had a scale from 0 to 100, with 0 as the pits and 100 as everything is fine, where are you on that scale to-day?' The scale is set up, 'in such a way that all the numbers are on the solution side' (de Shazer, 1994: 104) but it is impossible to be sure about what any number means, even for the client. They and we know that 50 is better than 40 and less good than 60, so answers provide a way of grading progress for both client and counsellor. But, more importantly, scaled questions and their answers help to make concrete what may be vague. The scale can vary as much as one wishes, for example 100 could represent the desired state at the end of counselling, or what the person would settle for, and so on.

Scales about *motivation* or willingness to work at the problem are also useful; for example, 'on a scale of 0 to 10, suppose 0 was you couldn't be bothered and 10 was you would do absolutely anything to deal with the problem, where are you on that scale to-day?' We also like to scale *confidence in one's ability* to act (optimism): 'on a scale of 1 to 10, if 1 was very little or no confidence that you can succeed and 10 was you are fully confident, where are you to-day?' We can then ask, 'how will life be when you move up from 3 to 4?', thereby helping the client to start constructing progressive change. The confidence scale also helps us to understand whether change is within the client's control. Scaled questions are important too in asking about danger or safety; for example, 'if 0 is the worst mother ever and 100 is a perfect Mum, how would you rate your mothering?' Because difference is the most valuable information for client and counsellor, we often ask, 'what will you be doing differently when you are one step higher?' Recognising difference means that these differences will make a difference.

Scales can also be used to compare how different people assess progress; it not being unusual for a complained-about client to underestimate support or overestimate confidence. For example, Alice and her daughter-in-law Beth were asked to assess Alice's rating of Beth's progress in making more friendly overtures towards Alice – but note their scores on paper and then share the results. Beth thought Alice would rate her at 2 and was surprised and delighted with Alice's 7. This led to a useful discussion about avoiding mind-reading, about asking simple questions, and about how difficult it is to guess another person's perceptions. However, with people who have come for counselling to please a partner and who may say they are at 10 already, the counsellor can ask, 'what would your partner say you were at?', and, 'what will she need to see you at so as to be able to take you back?' Or a client could be asked, 'between 1 and 10, how confident is your partner that you want to control your drinking?'

Even though we cannot be sure what a number means to a client, we can discuss the difference between numbers and so a bridge is created between client and counsellor. For example many clients think hard and then say, 'about half-way'. We find it useful to ask whether they are on the 49 or 51 side of halfway. A reply of the former suggests only a small movement is needed to get over the pivotal line, while a reply of 51 indicates that they are already over the line. Both replies can therefore be used to engender hope and set in motion small constructive change. With small children we draw sad and smiley faces at each end of the scale or simplify the scale to 0 = the worst, 5 = good enough and 10 = the very best. With slightly older children, other pictures can be used to generate some fun and take the heat out of a history of failure. For example, the scale could show a devil at one end and an angel at the other. This also helps both child and parents set attainable goals; it being obvious that no child can be expected to turn into an angel.

When clients report at subsequent sessions that they have moved up the scale, it is important not to launch too enthusiastically into cheering mode. We tend to convey our delight but check out the client's perception of progress by using a 'satisfaction with their score' scale. A low score on this indicates that they would prefer a more ambitious goal. Where they are satisfied, it is important to ask how they did it to strengthen the emergence of a new story of competence; what narrative therapists call 'thickening the counterplot'.

Thickening the counterplot

Freeman *et al.* (1997) point out that the problem-saturated story has mass and considerable evidence to support its momentum; especially where a 'diagnosis' has been seized upon as an explanation or excuse for behaviour. Thus simple reframes or positive statements by the counsellor are easily discounted and, 'an alternative story must be established in which the characters, their intentions, and their circumstances are as well developed, colorful, and convincing as the problem's' (Freeman *et al.*, 1997: 95). This alternative story is developed largely by asking, 'how did you do that?' and by beginning each subsequent session by asking, 'what's better?' instead of asking, 'what's happened?' (the latter tends to elicit more problem talk). The client's ability to repeat the competence is further encouraged by taking time to get as much detail as possible, asking what it says about the client's character and motivation, and so on. The plot is also strengthened by being told to other people. Even telling others of one's decision to change can help. We can discuss who would be the person most likely to believe it, how it could be broadcast more, and ask what advice the client would give to others with similar problems.

Also important is regular summarising to provide feedback. At the Milwaukee centre workers take a break and work up a verbal feedback that includes compliments and tasks from a reflecting team who have been watching the session from behind a screen. Few counsellors will have the luxury of a reflecting team but it is simple enough to pause, read through one's notes, and them summarise exceptions, abilities, solutions and so on. The process helps people to see aspects of reality that were ignored due to a focus on problems.

We like the Epston approach to written feedback (for a fuller discussion, see White and Epston, 1990) and we will be showing some examples of this in later chapters. After experimenting with narrative letters for clients, we expanded a recording format developed by Berg and Reuss (1998) to include as many elements of counterplot thickening as possible, posting a copy of this to the client. A covering letter which underlines our assumption that the client is the expert by asking them to check the accuracy of the notes is always sent. The notes include the following sections:

1   *Problem*   Here the current status of the difficulty is described, what has been happening, current worries, and wants.
2   *Exceptions/progress*   Lists of efforts made, achievements, differences, what others have done, scales can be mentioned, good ideas the client has had, things they have worked out.
3   *Thoughts on solutions*   What worked for the client. What s/he was

able to do and feel they can do. How they did it. What is useful. Any new ideas from the session.

4 *Homework* Tasks developed by the client and the worker in the session. These can end with the additional point: 'If x has some better ideas of his own he will do this instead'.

5 *Afterthoughts* These are any reflections and suggestions that come to the counsellor's mind after the session, such as compliments and new metaphors; a new task perhaps.

6 *Next appointment.*

The client's narrative is faithfully recorded but edited, or rather formatted by us, to separate *what* has been achieved (exceptions and progress) and *how* it was achieved (thoughts and solutions). This is to strengthen the counterplot. This written feedback is costly on our time but we feel it is worth at least an additional session in terms of thickening the counterplot, co-constructing the future free of the problem, and building on what the client brought to the session. Some clients never get letters, especially letters congratulating them on what they are doing and puzzling over how they do it. We find that clients keep these notes and re-read them over the period of the counselling. Because they are written in constructive language they are often shared by clients with others, such as parents. They also function as a constructive case record and are useful in supervision. Sadly, all too often, case records serve to construct the problem story more than the solution.

Tasks

The approach uses a set of special tasks, based on its basic assumptions. These are often developed with the client, who is invited to have a go or to experiment with them and keep track of any difference that is made. However, the invitation is a permissive one in that the clients can change the task or do something they have thought up or that might feel more useful. When they take notice of what difference is made, if this is valuable the task can be repeated, if not it can be changed. So there is no expectation that a task will be done. Tasks are couched in the client's language and may be metaphorical, behavioural or mental, although mental tasks seem to be more useful if they are made behavioural; for example, a task to notice differences can be put as noticing and making a list. The main tasks can be described as observational tasks, the F1 task, pretend tasks, prediction tasks, 'do something different' and 'do more of the same' tasks. We will consider each in turn.

An *observation task* is usually a request to notice aspects of one's own or of others' behaviour; for example, notice what you are doing that helps you to avoid drinking so that we can discuss these things next time. The task can bring more exceptions to light. The task can be anything that is done which is in the direction of the goal. Observing others is also useful; for example, 'observe what your teacher is doing that shows she is being helpful to you'. These tasks are often suggested in situations where the client has problems with other people and their motivation to make personal changes is low.

The *F1 task* is so called because it was (and still can be) used as a standard (formulaic) task in first sessions. It invites the client to note and list all the things that are happening in their life that they want to continue to happen. This is particularly useful if the goal is vague. It also aids motivation in reluctant clients as it seems to be more interested in what does not need to change. For example, Fred and Pauline wanted to regain their sex life which had been on hold whilst Pauline underwent chemotherapy. They had made sexual overtures to each other on several occasions but these had led to sex only on a relaxed afternoon when they were on holiday and not likely to be interrupted by unannounced, but welcome, visits from their large grown up family. Their homework task was outlined in their notes thus:

> Fred and Pauline will have to let some part of their busy family life go if they want sex back in their lives. The problem is which bit of their lives do they agree is less important than a good sex life? To help them find out − after all, they may have very different ideas about what is important − they will each make a list of what they do not want to change about their lives. They will then compare lists and see if they have any agreement. If there is no agreement, they can start negotiating about this. If they get stuck, they will ring for another appointment.

Pretend tasks are helpful for generating exceptions where the client is having difficulty in seeing any. When clients pretend to be less depressed they are likely to have a better week and be able to report some small changes. Is there any difference between pretending to be less depressed and being less depressed? Certainly others often cannot tell the difference and react with the person accordingly. Pretending to do is virtually the same as doing, it shows that one can do; de Shazer says that pretending

> serves to disconnect the solution construction and development process from the problem and to by-pass the client's historical, structural perspective and any disagreements about what the problem is. Once the solution develops . . . it no longer matters what the problem might have been. (1991: 114)

Berg and Reuss (1998) suggest that a coin toss is added to this task; for example, for women who cannot make a decision whether or not to leave an alcohol-addicted partner (the supposedly co-dependent woman). The coin determines on a particular day whether the woman is pretending that no matter what happens she will either leave her partner or stay with him and this gives her space to see how either decision would feel. We elaborate even further when using pretend tasks in order to address in a very small way feelings of powerlessness. We like to build up a story round the coin, asking the client to choose from a selection of foreign coins which one represents the place they would most like to visit when the problem is no longer there. When the pretend task is to have one day pretending, depending on the toss of the coin, that all their problems are solved or have an ordinary day, we also ask them to choose which side of the coin is the happiest side and nominate this as the problem-solved pretend day.

For people who say that they will find it difficult to pretend that their problems are solved, we combine the task with borrowing from a life they admire. For example, Lindsay wanted to 'be better' at school but didn't want to be seen as a swot on her pretend days. She identified another pupil who managed to combine 'being good' with being popular so Lindsay's task was to pretend to be this girl on the happy coin side days. What we most enjoy about this experiment is the number of times the coin seems to turn up on the favoured pretend days! Where there are relationship problems or complaints about behaviour, the complained-about person can be asked to pretend to be better some days and the complaining person asked to discern which days. This undermines the problem story as well as empowering the complained-about person to behave differently without losing face.

Prediction tasks are often used to develop some control over difficulties that seem to be beyond the client's control; for example, hearing

voices or having an urge to do something anti-social. People who practise predicting 'compulsiveness' can get more and more of their
predictions right; when they get most of them right we have proof of
some control. For example, David worried about drinking bouts that
led to violence but could not identify any control other than it depending on what mood he was in when he got up. He was given a
prediction chart and asked to consult his parents and girlfriend to see
if they too could predict good days and what they noticed differently
about him on those days. At his next appointment, he reported that
he had 'predicted' a bad day and worked out with his girlfriend how
to handle it differently. Again, as Kylie had a large file at her children's
home filled with details of misbehaviour, she was asked to undertake
a pretend task but also tell staff that she was doing a good and bad
behaviour experiment and ask them if they could predict which days
were likely to be which. This changed how they reacted with her.

'*Do something different*' tasks can be used when other tasks are
making no difference. They sound vague and they mean that the counsellor cannot find a specific task to suit, but they assume that the client
knows more than they think they know and any different tasks has a
better chance of success than one that is not helping. Experience shows
that clients often do find better ideas. On the other hand it may be
that it does not matter what the task is at times like this, so long as
it is different and one keeps track of the differences that follow. Maybe
changes merely need an opportunity to happen. After all, change is
constant and inevitable. Yet, to stop using failed solutions can be
difficult – the 'must try harder' attitude.

'*Do more of the same*' speaks for itself and obviously is suggested
when a task is working well, 'now that you know what works, do it
more'. When changes happen it can be useful to ask, 'how will you
know that this is not a fluke?' If there are no changes, the client can
be asked to take a step in a direction which will be good for them;
a vague task but still one that encourages them to do something
different. All these tasks promote a step forward in re-storying a life,
especially the conversation in which the differences are discussed.

Always we aim for transparency when we suggest homework. The
tasks arise from the messages given on existing solutions and those
identified during the session; and they are not delivered in an expert-
sounding way. We usually suggest them as experiments, explain the
rationale behind them, and are honest when we are not sure how they
work. For example, it was suggested that Carol – a particularly tal-

ented artist – might like to make an individualised dream catcher for her intrusive thoughts. She asked if this worked on a spiritual or a psychological level. After much thought, the counsellor said that she thought possibly both, although she had only considered a psychological level previously.

However carefully the homework tasks are negotiated, there is always the danger that the client will not feel powerful enough to reject the counsellor's suggestion, so it is stressed that homework is entirely voluntary. Most importantly, the client is told that if they have a better idea, then do this instead. Where the homework is not completed, resistance is not considered; it simply means that the counsellor did not understand well enough and must listen more carefully.

In conclusion, the approach:

- Believes people are multi-storied and endeavours to make the client the privileged author.
- Privileges people's lived experience and abilities.
- Encourages multiple perspectives and acts to deconstruct stories of 'expert knowledge'.
- Encourages a perception of change that is always possible.
- Encourages many possible futures through the co-construction of alternative stories.

The basic rules are:

- If its working, don't fix it.
- If it worked once, do it again.
- If actions are not working, do something different.

We have found that getting detailed pictures of goals, of life after the solution, and scaling *both* motivation and confidence in one's ability, are key techniques.

4

The first session

Using the space between setting a date and the first session

Problem-focused counselling is usually delivered within a framework of hour-long weekly sessions with the number of sessions agreed established either at the point of referral or the first session. This involves the counsellor in making some sort of diagnosis – even though Rogers has said that this is not necessary. Even Kahn's 'middle way between the schools of warm support and those of neutral transference analysis . . .' accepts that there will be continual, automatic diagnosis and that 'all people with emotional problems suffer from deficits of the self and could benefit from . . . empathic therapy' (Kahn, 1997: 175). In most problem-focused counselling the therapeutic relationship is seen as different from all others the client engages in as the hour-long session distances the client from other relationships and heightens that with the counsellor, thus there is great emphasis on the importance of the therapist in the client's life. This results in concern over how not only transference is handled but also endings. Winnicott described this relationship as resembling the primary maternal relationship:

> in which the mother is something for the infant more than she does for him. Without actually establishing a regressed mother–infant relationship, a counsellor can meet the fundamental needs for that relatedness and for the space within which personal exploration and discovery can go on without interference from 'grown-up' demands and consequences. (Noonan, 1983: 65–6)

Thus the client attending a first session with a problem-focused counsellor enters a sort of expert black box which will frame the encounter, diagnose the problem, and begin work on personal change. But a counsellor working from a basis of solution talk does not see herself as holding this sort of expertise; she does not have to wait until the first meeting for any of these elements to begin happening. By taking what the client says at face value, she assumes that the request for an appointment signals 'engagement' – that engagement has already occurred; that is, she takes seriously the client's intention to 'do something' about what is bothering them and makes no assumptions about ambivalence or possible resistance to the therapeutic encounter.

This means that the time between making the appointment and arriving for the first appointment is seen as an important period of change. It could not be otherwise because, as de Shazer (1988) maintains, there is no problem that is always happening. In this period there is often some positive move towards alleviating the influence of the problem on the person, even if it is only a thinking through of the story to be presented at the first session. Solution-focused counsellors take this idea even further, asking clients to note any change in this period and asking them about it at the first session. Sometimes clients use this period so constructively that they arrive with their problems solved. Problem-focused counsellors would see this as worrying evidence of 'flight into health' as they hold an assumption that:

> Because enduring change in behaviour involves alterations in the unconscious inner world and this threatens the client's defensive solutions to his anxieties, counselling is often slow, painful and resisted. (Noonan, 1983: 48)

We differ completely on this point and consider it a matter for celebration when clients arrive with their problems solved, although they might make good use of a couple of sessions to strengthen the counterplot through telling and retelling. For example, Katy had done a lot of thinking in the period between a brief informal chat to see if the counselling service was for her and attending the first session. She arrived at her first session with her preferred solution well worked out so no assessment of her goals was undertaken; the session being used to provide her with an opportunity to identify her strengths and tell how she would 'do' her solution. The new plot was thickened by posting her a copy of the counsellor's session notes (carefully using the client's own words), see below:

PROBLEM

Katy would like to get more confidence in herself and not believe that she is always in the wrong at home or that she has to keep doing things to please people. Her mum is very stressed with looking after five children and takes amphetemines sometimes and smokes cannabis most days. She relies on Katy to help her more than Katy feels able to do. Katy's mum is proud of how Katy sticks by her and helps but doesn't tell her other things she is proud of. Katy is proud of her mum for bringing them up all on her own.

EXCEPTIONS/PROGRESS

1   Katy rates herself at 51% on the 'best person she could be' scale. She used to be higher than this when she didn't have two little sisters or her mum taking drugs. Then she felt good about herself all the time.

2   Since visiting the project, Katy has taken more notice of herself, not thinking as much about how to please other people all the time. She has been getting on better with mum and feeling better about herself.

3   Although her mum doesn't always show that she appreciates Katy, her dad does – even if this is by sending presents instead of saying the words.

4   Despite all Katy's extra work, she still manages to go to the youth centre and give talks. She has won many awards.

5   Katy had a difficult time when she was thirteen (doing gas, shop lifting, etc.) but she has turned her life round and doesn't do stuff like this anymore.

6   Katy has kept her school work going well. She is doing her exams at the moment and has a place to go to college.

THOUGHTS ON SOLUTIONS

1   After visiting the project, Katy tried to explain herself to her mum instead of shouting with her. That worked a bit.

2   Katy has good ideas about how much responsibility she should take as a sixteen-year-old. She reckons she should clean her bedroom and help with the washing up, cook her mum a special meal once a week to give her a break, look after the little ones at weekends so that her mum can go out, iron her own clothes, organise her school work by doing revision and setting the alarm clock, keep up her part-time job and save money for when

she goes to college as mum is on benefits, go out with friends each night during the holidays, come in earlier when she has school or college work to do and so as not to wake the little ones.

3 Katy got over her early difficulties by going to the youth centre and putting her skills to good use. She can express herself well. Katy is an exceptional person who has survived a difficult upbringing; she should do very well on her college course.

HOMEWORK
Katy has made a good start on getting her problems sorted so she will do more of the same — it's working! As well, she will sit down with her mum and go through her list of reasonable responsibilities so that she and mum can come to a sensible arrangement about what can be expected.

Katy attended a further two sessions to tell how well her solution had worked and describe how she did it in detail. Problem-focused counsellors might think that the problems were insufficiently addressed and would resurface but, as solution-talk counselling has no notion of 'closure', Katy can return at any time if she needs further help. A few people do return to counselling later on. In brief counselling, however, it is not uncommon for people to finish after one session and there is growing evidence for the effectiveness of single-session counselling, especially where the time between making and keeping the appointment has resulted in workable solutions (see for example Miller, Hubble and Duncan, 1996). When Talmon (1990) began to use a solution-focused approach he assumed when people did not return for a second session that they had dropped out. But on researching this he discovered that many had achieved their goal as a result of a single session. Such we believe is the power of solution talk in which people can quickly *experience* change. We find the long-term effectiveness of one or two sessions is confirmed by letters telling of happiness and success we receive many months after the event.

Setting the scene

Important though it is to provide a welcoming and comfortable environment, it is also essential to address power issues at the first session so that clients can feel they have control over events and can make decisions and choices. The main way this is done is by making the process transparent. As we will be hoping to convey to the client that we value their ideas and that they will have a major say in the process, we begin with introductions that aim to demystify counselling. For example, we usually ask clients what expectations they have of what counselling will be like, as well as what they hope it will achieve. We consider this more important than beginning with the person-centred recommended, 'how can I best help you?'; especially as Mearns and Thorne (1999) say that 'it is important to respond to the feelings behind the question when clients ask what [counsellors] do' (1997 edn: 102). Client expectations might be culled from previous experiences of counselling, from consulting friends, or from watching television programmes. They almost always say that they expect to talk about their problems; not infrequently followed up by a statement to the effect that they find this hard to do.

Rather than view this as resistance or ambivalence, we honour their courage in being able to come and then explain our approach; saying that we are much more interested in where they are going than where they have been as the past can't be changed, and is this okay for them? If they answer in the affirmative, we then say that this means that they can talk about their problems if they want to do so but, equally, they don't have to talk about their problems if they don't want to. We also add that we will be asking some pretty crazy questions, so how will they tell us when they don't want to answer a question? This helps establish a 'pass' convention and saves much time trying to interpret non-verbal language, such as gazing fixedly at their shoes. It is important to provide a test or invitation for this convention early on to show that you do actually mean it; for example, 'that was a deeply personal question. Remember you can tell me to mind my own business.' Having a 'pass' convention also solves the counsellor's potential problems over how much to self-disclose in response to clients' questions about the counsellor's life.

We also emphasise that we value their opinions and ideas and hope that they will tell us if we seem not to be understanding them properly. This is done by regularly saying, 'it seems to me that you . . . or have I got it completely wrong?', or by acknowledging that we meet a lot of people who *seem* to have the same problem but that they are all very different so they will need to tell us what these differences are. Where there is an ethnic or gender gap, the difference is bridged by adding that we cannot truthfully say we understand how it feels from a black or white or male or female perspective, so will they please remember to keep educating us. Differences of sexuality are also discussed, although we have found that clients involved in same-sex violence often prefer to be seen by a heterosexual counsellor because their networks are so small that confidentiality and safety can be problematic. For example, Monica could not turn to a specialist lesbian counselling service as her violent partner worked there. Nor could she consider a place at the local women's refuge as it was run by a friend who knew nothing about the violence she was experiencing. That this is not an unusual situation, see also Renzetti (1992) and Walsh (1999).

Then we discuss the format of sessions, saying that an hour is usual because that is how long most people can concentrate but that they can leave earlier if they want, or take a break. To empower children (age is a difference which is hard to bridge), we add a rule that no-one in the room is allowed to say anything about the young person other than good things whilst they are out of the room. As young people frequently take the opportunity to leave the room when they have heard enough from a parent or carer about their shortcomings, this rule is extremely useful. The young person who leaves the room to avoid being flooded with negative messages about themselves usually hovers outside the door to hear if, indeed, good things are being said about them. Parents of 'complained-about' children are encouraged to do this by asking what makes them proud of their child. This ensures that young people soon come back in to the room, and increases their involvement in the session. With young people, confidentiality limits are illustrated with an example of the sorts of situations which would mean that social services or the police had to be informed.

Checked out at this information-giving stage is that the agency information pack has been received and understood. It also helps the client to begin to feel that they will be able to make choices about the course of counselling by reminding them that at the end of the session they will have several choices: they can return for another session if one is needed – always emphasising that counselling is not necessarily a lengthy process; they can change to another counsellor if they would prefer a different approach to their problem; or they can decide that counselling is not for them. We are not precious about the relationship and really do not mind if they want a change, so there is no interpreting this as resistance or insisting that they work through any rejection of us. Neither do we mind if they are also seeking help elsewhere as we find it quite reasonable for people to consult a wide range of people over their difficulties; although psychodynamic-oriented counsellors do seem to find this problematic.

We suspect that problem-focused counsellors do not aim for such transparency as an explanation of their beliefs and values would probably offend the client. For example, imagine how you would feel if this systemic family therapist came clean about her underlying assumptions about your request for counselling:

> despite verbal protestations to the contrary, the family's attitude towards change will be almost wholly negative, since symptomatology is the means whereby the family's homeostasis is maintained. The family's interaction during the first encounter with the therapist will, to a greater or lesser extent, be directed towards meeting its unconscious need to overthrow the therapist's efforts to act as therapist . . . Inevitably, therefore, there has to be some kind of struggle between the family and the therapist commencing at the outset of the first interview. (Walrond-Skinner, 1976: 37)

Or how would you feel if a psychotherapist informed you of his assumptions about transference and his role as mother figure:

> The psychoanalytic setting is a frame for unanticipated invitations. And these attributions of apparent sexual identity bring with them a largely unconscious repertoire of permissions and prohibitions to act, of wished-up assumptions of sexual entitlement . . . despite the inevitable vagaries of the patient's transference the analyst always knows fundamentally that he will be experienced as at the 'deepest' levels of the patient's personality. (Phillips, 1993: 108)

It seems odd to us that problem-focused counsellors aim for congruence and genuiness on the one hand but, on the other, withhold their basic assumptions about the nature of people from the very people they are attempting to empower. Writing down these assumptions in case notes further constructs the client within an expert and hidden narrative, capturing and fixing a 'thin' description of the person which cannot be challenged (White and Epston, 1990). To demonstrate transparency further, we not only explain our assumptions but say that what we are writing down in the session will be typed up later and that the client will get a copy of this for information and accuracy-checking; that one copy will go on file; and that the only other person who will see it will be the supervisor, who will only know the client's first name. We emphasise that supervision is a check on the counsellor and usually say what the supervisor is called to make more real the fact that there will be two minds concentrating on the problem. Writing down what the client says and discussing how this material will be studied by us helps to show clients that they are taken seriously.

This is a good point at which to show the client the case file and give them the opportunity to read the referral form. If it is a self-referral they can comment on any change that has taken place since making the appointment. If the client has been referred by another person, the counsellor can check for factual accuracy and perceptions about the nature of the problem. A referral by someone other than the client is simply that person's *version* of the story and it is important not to join with the referrer in entering the client into a 'thin' story. These are usually pathological stories which conflate the person with the problem. For example, if the referral is made by a family member, it will often describe the client's perceived deficiencies in family functioning. If it is made by a professional, it is likely to be couched in the sort of language that the referrer thinks is suitable to meet the professional criteria for acceptance for counselling and will use pathological descriptions such as, 'he is eneuretic', 'she is depressed', 'she has an anxious attachment to her mother'. When people are entered into other people's stories, particularly where they 'fit' with dominant narratives, the client will quickly come to believe that they *are* a problem.

Discussing the words used in the referral is the beginning of a narrative conversation in which we are aiming to 'thicken' the client's story and move away from the 'thin' description contained in the referral (Payne, 2000). Thin, pathological stories limit possibilities for client action because they fix people in small boxes, from which they will then need help to escape. Through an early discussion of terms such as lethargic, depressed, violent, auditory hallucinations and so forth, a richer description can be obtained. For example, the counsellor can ask, 'how do you do depression?' or, 'it says here, you lack skills in face-to-face socialising. What does this mean?' or, 'what do you do when you hear voices?' Exceptions often emerge at this point; for example, the client may tell you that they argue with their voices and resist their instructions or that they only 'do temper' when they are wound up by other pupils at school. Where exceptions are not evident you can begin to discuss the influence of dominant narratives on the maintenance of the influence of the problem in their lives; for example, with young people who are repeatedly rejected by their parents and see themselves as unloveable, you could possibly question the supposedly fundamental nature of mother-love by saying something like, 'we can't choose our parents and it doesn't seem that you were at the front of the queue when parents were given out . . .'. If the client agrees that the referral is an accurate description of their life, you can them move on to take a fuller history which reduces helplessness and feelings of failure (Dolan, 1998).

History-taking and goal-setting

Having carefully completed introductions and explanations, a useful starting point for taking a history is to ask a 'worthwhile question' to begin goal-setting; such as, 'what needs to happen to make it worthwhile your giving up an hour of your time and taking three buses to get here?' We tend to follow the format of solution-focused counselling as a general guide to the session but use ideas from narrative counselling to add richer detail. Much depends on where the problem is embedded; whether it seems to reside mainly in interpersonal relationships over which the client has a sense of control and influence, or whether these relationships are more influenced by dominant narratives.

On paper, Avril's problem looked complex – she had been raped at a young age and later became reluctant to go to school, became preoccupied with her health, and then developed eating difficulties in early adolescence. She had been receiving counselling for the school problems from an educational social worker, whom she found helpful, and attended an adolescent mental health service for help with the eating difficulties. After several sessions with a clinical psychologist, she refused further appointments as these focused on her experiences of rape and she wanted to talk about her eating difficulties.

Avril's answer to the worthwhile question revealed clear goals; staying 'on the surface' and following the format of the solution-focused approach was sufficient to identify workable solutions. Exceptions to her difficulties were easily elicited; she knew 'how she did them'; and she also 'knew this about herself', so there was no need to deconstruct the problem to examine the possible influence of dominant narratives around eating and dieting. Avril was also comfortable with this approach which respected her decision to change counsellor so that she could choose her own goals and solutions. She began the session by referring many of the questions on a 'recovery chart' (see Appendix 3b) to her mother on the grounds that, 'mum knows me better than I do myself', but spoke for herself when asked 'how she did it' (the exceptions), as she was the only person who knew this. She became visibly more confident as the session progressed, suggesting several possible ways of 'doing' her solution. Narrative techniques were used only in the preparation of her notes; written communications being an important way of opening up possibilities and 'thickening' the solution story (for a discussion of narrative letters to clients, see Freeman *et al.*, 1987; Epston, 1998). We use letters and certificates but find that our adaptation of Berg and Reuss's (1998) session notes for the file are appropriate for both the file and client copy, as long as care is taken in the composition of the covering letter: see below.

SESSION NOTES

Name: Avril   Date: July 2000

PROBLEM
Avril has problems with sleeping, eating, feeling part of a family, standing up for herself, tolerating criticism, and intrusive thoughts. She thinks some of these might be to do with a rape experience when she was young and family problems but they are tied up with teenage issues too. At the moment, eating properly is her main problem. Avril is 5' 5" and 7 stone but she would like to be 8 stone. She would like to gain this weight in 4–5 months. She would also like to be getting out of the house more and spending more time with dad.

EXCEPTIONS/PROGRESS
1 Avril has made a lot of progress recently. She has started going to school regularly, resisting self-harm, and taking safety measures. She rates herself at 51 on the 'happiness' scale and is a lot closer to 100 on the 'best person she could be' scale. This means that this is probably a very good time for Avril to start counselling again as she is able to work from her strengths.
2 She wasn't able to eat in front of people at all but can now eat in front of a whole roomful of people at school; in front of her dad and his family; and in front of her mum.

THOUGHTS ON SOLUTIONS

1   Avril is not sure how she made the recent progress but it must have been growing steadily because she rates herself at 'pretty much' or 'very much' on being able to talk about what happened; able to talk about other things; keeping smart; being able to leave the house; going to social events (when she gets the opportunity); being interested in the future (a very good sign); choosing supportive relationships; and liking herself. This is an impressive list of achievements and Judith would be interested to hear Avril's thoughts about how she might have done it (good ideas come in very useful in counselling).

2   Avril did the eating in front of people by taking a big plunge. Although she started off with a bag of crisps and worked up to full meal, she just made the decision to walk into the dining room and start eating. It only took her half a term to work up to a full meal.

HOMEWORK

1   Avril will either eat one whole meal on Saturdays in front of her mum, mum's partner, and her boyfriend Darren or she will toss a coin to decide whether she is having a pretend eating day or an ordinary day. As she hopes to put on weight quickly, she will change her diet and have lots of cheese, milk and fibre. Mum and her partner are on a diet so they will have different food. Mum will cook because Avril says she does better meals but, some days, Avril will prepare a simple meal for herself.

2   Mum has been worrying about Avril's eating and asking lots of questions (being a proper mum!) but she thinks she will do something different. She will ask Avril what she wants for her tea when she comes home from school and then Avril will probably tell her what she ate for lunch without having to be asked.

3   They will all have a treat one a week. This will probably be a takeaway cheeseburger and chips. Mum's partner will pay for this.

4   Avril, mum and her partner have had a lot of stress in their lives. They have coped with it well but Judith wonders if they have missed out on having family fun. They might talk about how to have family fun that doesn't cost too much. Avril remembers enjoying playing Monopoly.

Date and time of next appointment: Avril thinks it will take about three weeks to do the eating experiments so she will report back in August.

Covering letter:

Dear Avril

As promised, here is a copy of your notes. I hope that I have got everything right but, if not, please let me know next time we meet so that I can make any necessary alterations. I have a feeling that I have forgotten some of your strengths – it did turn out to be a long list. I am amazed at what you have achieved over such a short time after the difficult times you have had.

I look forward to hearing how the eating experiments go but, remember, if you have a better idea about how to do them, then do that instead. You may not know how you made all that progress at the moment but you must have been doing something right. When you work out what this is, then do more of it.

I did enjoy talking with you and your mum. It makes my job so much easier when I meet with families where there is such a lot of care and concern.

In Shane's case, a more reflective approach was used, despite him having clear goals: he wanted

to be working, being my normal self. No worries on my mind. A normal seventeen-year-old who gets up and goes to work. Sees his mates at the weekend [looking at the referral form written by his youth offending team worker] That's it, my temper. As soon as the fuse goes, I want to lash out. I go out and calm down, come back and it starts again. I'm not bothered for me but I've got a four-year-old nephew thinks the world of me. Do it for him, not be a waster.

There were lots of exceptions but as soon as the counsellor began to look at his strengths (we usually change tack and move from the problem by saying something like, 'we've talked a lot about your temper, can you tell me some good things about yourself?'), the violence that went with Shane's temper emerged as a bad influence on his good points: 'I've got a big heart, too big . . . I like to get on with people, have a good social life, always there to lend a hand . . . whether it's to talk or *do* something . . . I'm getting older, not as much of a softie as I was. I scare myself sometimes.'

It would have been quite possible to pursue exceptions but his answers revealed that he was surrounded by violence and it seemed more appropriate to deconstruct the problem and identify unique outcomes via addressing the dominant narrative influencing his violence. This was done by asking him what sort of man he is:

> *Shane:* I can look after myself. I've got the muscle. Only just started . . . getting more confident and it just . . . I don't like it. Someday I'll come up against someone bigger and better . . . I would like to be someone who can look after himself and his family. Basically like my dad. He's had a hard life but he's come out on top. But he's not in control of his temper when he's had a bit of beer. [The counsellor introduces a family differentiation exercise (Dolan, 1998: 126).] I do want to be like my dad but I don't want to be like his temper. He looks small but he can do some damage.
>
> *Counsellor:* What bits of dad do you want to keep?
>
> *Shane:* My temper, that goes straight out of the window. Keep my sense of humour. Me dad has this too.

The violence is then mapped (for a fuller discussion, see Denborough, 1996) by asking who wins and who loses when he fights, beginning with dad:

> *Shane:* He would win physically. Dad would win the emotional fight and mum would get the heartache. If we fight, we all lose something.
>
> *Counsellor:* How could you have a win/win situation?
>
> *Shane:* When mum takes one of our sides . . . or stop and think about what we're doing. We've done that. Had a chat and come back. We have arguments all the time but I always manage to go back. If I left the house, I'd be a lot better. I'd like to be independent but I need a job first. Then in the next two years I can be having that conversation with my dad.

As he cannot leave home at the moment, the temper is studied as a preliminary to externalising it. He describes it as a red bomb:

Counsellor: It looks to me as though it's an heirloom. Do you know what an heirloom is?
Shane: Yes. Something that gets passed down the family.
Counsellor: And you want to stop it getting passed down any further?
Shane: YES! Then my kids won't get it.

Shane's 'homework' consisted of asking him to explore the dominant story further by asking him to study the family heirloom and see what works best to defuse the bomb and what works less well – he had identified an ability to stop and think about what he is doing so this competency is built upon.

Setting tasks to strengthen solutions

As can be seen from these two examples, a combination of appropriate tasks was suggested through the identification of exceptions and solutions. In Avril's case, these consisted of a straightforward task (doing more of what was already working), and a pretend task (to extend a successful solution to another setting without risking failure). Mum was asked to 'do something different' as constantly checking on Avril's eating away from home, although an understandable concern, increased Avril's difficulties in eating at home. Because Shane's story was saturated in family and community violence, he was asked to study the influence of the problem on him at the same time as his unique outcome, stopping and thinking, was built into a task which would enable him to repeat it.

Where clients are particularly disempowered, with concommitant safety issues, we adapt the standard F1 task in line with narrative ideas about the influence of dominant stories about family life. For example, following the death of her husband, Lena was dependent on her teenage son for most of her physical care. She had several hospital admissions following overdoses and falls and her current admission raised safety concerns as she had a black eye. She had complained to neighbours previously that her son hit her but denied this in hospital. She both loved and feared her son and was confused about how she wanted to live her life. In this instance, asking her what she didn't want to change would not have been helpful as most things were outside her control, so her homework was designed to provide her with opportunities to make choices by increasing the likelihood of other people in her life taking some responsibility:

POSSIBLE SOLUTIONS
Lena has thought out the solutions for her safety and come up with three possible answers:

1   She could move to a two-bedroomed house with her son, Mark. This would resolve the overcrowding but Lena couldn't manage the stairs. She doesn't want a flat. Anyway, she likes her own bungalow when she has it all to herself.
2   She could move to sheltered accommodation and Mark keep the bungalow. Lena has thought about this quite a lot recently but it would mean leaving her own home. It might also be a problem for Mark as he already owes rent arrears on his old flat.
3   Mark could move out of the bungalow and sleep on someone else's sofa while he pays off his rent arrears. This would be the best solution for Lena's safety and health but it is the hardest one to do. She doesn't think Mark would agree to move and she would worry if they fell out as he is all she has left.

ACTION TAKEN
None at the moment until Lena is sure what will be best for her safety. It is difficult to make any decision about one's grown-up children, especially as Lena has lost her husband. She has another appointment next week to talk about it some more.

AFTERTHOUGHTS
There does seem to be a lot of confusion in Lena's bungalow. Mark is shouting one moment and cuddling his mum the next. Lena is hoping he will be grown up and get his own place but she also likes him around when he is being thoughtful. This can't make decision-making about safety easy for either of them. Judith did wonder if it would help if Mark was asked how he rates his mum's safety? Perhaps we could ask him how she could be more safe? Judith wonders if there is anything different he could do that would make his mum safer?
Also, what would Lena's carers or her friend say would make her safe?

Lena showed Mark her copy of the notes and he agreed to become involved in the counselling. Together they quickly devised a safety plan which had benefits for both of them: they would live separately but close enough to maintain regular contact. Whilst waiting for rehousing, Mark developed a plan to extend his exceptions to hitting Lena.

Sometimes safety issues are not so obvious but become clearer when an attempt is made to clarify vague goals by asking the client to write a letter from the future – not for posting (Dolan, 1998: 77). This is a particularly useful alternative when scaled and miracle questions have failed to elicit any detail. For example, the three Duffy children were referred for assistance in coming to terms with their mixed feelings about their father leaving the home after a long period of domestic violence. Their letters from the future revealed that they would be living with their mother but that she would not be drinking – a fact of their lives which hadn't been known previously.

For complained-about children, who not infrequently have no clear goals because they want everything to change, we often give them a notebook to take home or to school asking for comments about the child. The writer is instructed to write anything good they have noticed about the child at the front of the book and anything bad at the back of the book. The latter entry has a rider: the writer is instructed not to write anything in this section of the book until they have written something in the front section. This politely empowers the child to approach the adult who they feel is picking on them the most.

Evaluating the session so far, and ending it

Where the homework task is simply 'do more of it', there is frequently no need for a second session so we always ask if the client thinks they will need a second session. Sometimes they wish to report on successes, sometimes successes need strengthening through telling; and sometimes minor adjustments are necessary but, as a general rule, we never commit ourselves – or clients – to a set number of sessions. Quite simply, the counselling process takes as long as it takes, although it is often brief. Clients can be surprised that they have solved their problems quickly (the influence of dominant narratives around counselling), but the necessity for further sessions is clarified by asking the client how they will know their problems have been solved; what they will be doing differently; and what other will people notice.

Neither is counselling necessarily a weekly activity. This can be burdensome for clients, who may wish to space their discussion of painful issues or whose progress may well not be even – it is discouraging not to have any progress to report. Where a second session is obviously indicated, we tend to consult with the client over how long they think it will take to do the tasks and set the next date accordingly. Where they are unsure, we ask them to ring for an appointment when they think they are ready, although we always add that appointments can be brought forwards or put back as necessary. Careful spacing of sessions with the client appears to reduce the overall number required.

Also important at this stage of the first session is evaluating with the client how useful the session has been, whether it was what they expected, and what would have been more useful. Clients are invariably polite when asked these questions so we build in checks against any complacency on our part. For example if the client says, 'it was a bit helpful', we add, 'oh dear, that's not good enough. What would I have been doing differently if I had been more helpful?' We also make it plain that our notes are open for revision and that the client can add any ideas, clarify our thinking about their problem and solutions, and correct inaccuracies. This is followed up in the covering letter accompanying the session notes. We find that young people are the most likely to request amendments, usually simple matters of detail; and sometimes clients whose cultural realities are different. For example, Indira requested numerous detailed changes to the notes outlining her tangled dowry arrangements but no changes to the comments about her emotional response to these. We always make these corrections in view of the client at subsequent sessions and send out amended notes. In this way, we hope to be no more than an influential part in the co-authoring of new life stories, not experts in other people's lives.

Reflecting on the first session

With practice we find that we can set out the notes for posting from our handwritten notes. The preparation of feedback notes involves a refocusing on strengths, unique outcomes and exceptions as well as paying further attention to the client's language, so it can be used in co-constructing the future story. Unless one has an excellent memory this needs to be done soon after the session, even if one has copious notes, and the doing of it requires considerable care as the formatting may need to reframe positively and underline what at first sight may seem like throw-away remarks.

When this process does not flow easily, we type out the verbatim notes for supervision. This enables reflection particularly on goal-setting, the possibility of more scaling questions and the pace of the work. Where a session drifts or goes round in circles, or fails to elicit either a clear problem or a clear solution story, we need to check out the basics: what did the client want, what do others want, who is the client or do we have a client? Difficulties are often linked to there being a difference between the complaint that is first expressed and what is wanted now, the complaint sometimes being just a ticket to counselling for something else, or a difference between the absence of the problem and the eventual solution. It is not easy to keep in mind that the relationship between the problem and the solution is always nominal. Neither is it easy to avoid digging around in the problem drawer when we need to be searching in the solution drawer; it is hard to transfer our curiosity to the solution, going back again and again to the future when the client will be getting by, happy or will have achieved their goal.

Sessions that feel stuck are often sessions where the worker has moved ahead of the client in one of two ways; by coming to a conclusion about the nature of the problem or the person, or by proposing various logical tasks for solution development. Although we distrust hypotheses about the nature or cause of difficulties, we can be lured at times into marrying our own explanations and logic, thereby losing the sense of uncertainty and puzzlement. Not unnaturally, the more stuck one feels the more one grasps at false certainties which cause us to part company with the client.

Scaling questions can feel tedious at times, especially when we get several 'don't knows', but, again, we risk losing the client if we underuse them. Along with the miracle question for developing clear goals, they rank as the main bridge between counsellor and client, 'providing a way of talking about things that are hard to describe – including progress toward the client's solution' (de Shazer, 1994: 92). De Shazer (1994) shows how slowly and thoroughly he uses them to develop 'creative misunderstandings' of what can be indescribable issues. Above all, patient scaling keeps the counsellor on the surface. If the client is talking about being unable to relax we need 'success at relaxing' scales; if the client is doing violence we need 'success at self-calming' scales. Note the use of verbs in preference to nouns; when the problem or the solution is framed as a noun it becomes more stuck and given; where it is framed as a verb it is more changeable and the client has greater possibility of personal agency or control.

Finally, the pace of the work needs to slow in proportion to its difficulty. We need to slowly ask for more and more information about goals, exceptions and solutions, 'refusing to take anything on trust alone, which sometimes means asking what are apparently stupid questions' (de Shazer 1994: 111). But this needs to be done following what de Shazer calls the 'principle of charity'; that is, assuming that people's ways of making sense of life are not very different from our own and assuming that it is as important for them as it is for us to get some agreement on the significance of what is being talked about, and to take it seriously.

Supervision

Solution-focused supervision often tends to be live. O'Connell (1998) suggests that this developed from a tradition of co-working in which counsellors learn 'on the job' with instant feedback from colleagues. This supportive learning reduces the need for one-to-one supervision but not every counsellor has the advantage of a reflecting team. Where one-to-one supervision is provided, it closely follows the approach taken with clients (for a fuller discussion, see Thomas, 1996, 2000).

In conclusion, we have three main concerns in a first session:

- What the client can tell us about what will be useful to them.
- What can they reasonably hope for.
- What ought we to do or not do.

5

Subsequent sessions

Because we have no fixed notion of what people should be like when they are better and, therefore, make no estimates about the number of sessions it might take before they reach their goals, each session is potentially the last session. The format of looking for exceptions/unique outcomes and progress, exploring possible solutions, summarising and negotiating homework is essentially the same in each session. The main thing that is different in subsequent sessions is that the problem is not necessarily revisited; it being more important to get into exception-finding to underline progress. We do this by asking an opening question that presumes there will have been positive change; usually a version of 'what's better?'.

What's better?

Clients are often a little puzzled or surprised with this opening as they expect to talk about their problems. The question is deliberately vague and therefore may lead to talking about areas of the client's life that may be seen as not directly related to the problem. More importantly it conveys an expectation that progress can be rapid or at least that some slight progress will begin to happen soon, thus it challenges the assumption many clients have that their problems will be always, or for quite a long time, with them (de Shazer, 1991: 103). Part of what makes a problem a Problem is that it is seen as always happening, 'the same damn thing over and over', whereas a mix of difficulties can be seen as just 'one damn thing after another', which is part and parcel of ordinary life, so we look for any sort of small or subtle change to counter the 'always happening' assumption.

We quite deliberately avoid saying things like, 'how are you?, how are things?, what's happened since we last met?', because these questions all encourage problem talk and diminish telling of successes. Asking 'what's better?' shows that we are interested in what has gone well in a client's life. This is an essential part of empowerment; emphasising that we believe that clients can, at least gradually, increase control over their lives; that they have lives where change happens between sessions rather than during them; and that they – not us – are the experts in these lives. Whilst we are willing to listen to their hardships and do not underestimate how difficult life can be for many clients, we wish to maintain a focus on solution-finding, amplifying any successes or exceptions – however small. This builds on de Shazer's (1994: 135) proposal that the work in subsequent sessions entails:

- constructing the interval between sessions as including improvement;
- checking on whether what the client did in the meantime is seen as useful, inviting the client to see things as improved;
- helping the client to figure out what he or she has done that led to the change so that they can see what to do more of;
- deciding whether the improvements are good enough;
- when no improvements can be found, working out how to do something different so as to avoid repeating what does not work.

The construction of the interval as 'things getting better' is done by discovering any small piece of change, discussing how the client did it, what and who helped, and what difference it made. The difference is scaled, comparing the good days with the less good or scaling aspects of the change. Selekman (1997) suggests that in all subsequent meetings there are four main possibilities: things are either better, the same, worse, or mixed.

When things are better

Not infrequently, there has been a large amount of progress and the client is bursting to report this. Whilst we are as delighted about this as the client, it is important not to say simply, 'well done', and move on to other topics. We ask detailed questions about the success in order to reveal *how* they did it so that it will be easier to do it again. For example, Avril came to her second session with her boyfriend rather than her mum and responded to, 'what's better?' with, 'lots of things'. She then smiled. The counsellor waited for more but only got, 'everything's better'. More puzzlement and a few prompts revealed that she had not only managed to eat in front of people but she had been eating more in both range and quantity of foods; this information being supplied by her boyfriend. Having elicited details about her improved eating, her general sense of well-being was checked out by asking her to rate herself on a 'happiness' scale. This showed an improvement but not perhaps so much as would have been expected by her delight in her eating achievements so she was asked to rate herself on a, 'how satisfied are you with this score?' scale to find out which goals still needed to be fulfilled and prevent premature 'cheering on of change'. As mentioned earlier, clients often have large and ambitious goals and it is important for us not to lower these by expressing our satisfaction with small progress before checking out that the client sees this as sufficient progress.

Avril said that she was not very satisfied as she felt that some days were better than others and then began problem talk about her bad days. Her boyfriend challenged this part of the conversation, commenting that there had been more good days than bad days. We often find that other people in the session start using solution talk more quickly than clients; indeed, we have found it a good indicator of strong and positive relationships when the other person has more interest in solutions than problems. The 'friend' who often accompanies a client at the first session, and is said to always 'be there for them', often disappears when there is no more misery to pick over. Darren's challenging of Avril's problem talk led the conversation on to what she was doing differently on good days and how she could do more of this. Much of this was to do with improving her social life, something she was ready for but about which her mother had doubts – Avril had previously responded to the damaging effects of the rape on her pride in her body by putting herself in dangerous social situations. This, in turn, led to Avril sorting out what she had meant in the first session when she said the rape was mixed up with teenage things.

Those readers who hypothesised in the previous chapter that Avril's request for a change of counsellor because she did not want to talk about the rape and had concerns that, if ignored, it would go underground and resurface in other forms of dysfunctional behaviour, will hopefully be reassured at this point. Avril brought the subject up herself when it became relevant to what she wanted to talk about, demonstrating how a preoccupation with past events can miss the complexities of the differing influences of the problem on people as they change and develop. The counsellor still stayed on the surface, Avril being most concerned about how the rape experience had different effects on her and her mum. She said her mum, not unnaturally, remained concerned about safety issues; whereas Avril felt that she had outgrown these and was more concerned about her disturbed sleep patterns – intrusive thoughts were preventing her from getting off to sleep. Detailed questions to elicit exceptions were asked; what had she tried and what worked. As all the things she had tried worked only partially, the counsellor told her some things which other young women had done as part of their sleep recovery from the intrusive effects of rape. These were offered as tentative suggestions which she might tailor to her own needs and which offered her the opportunity to explore her own solution-finding more thoroughly. For example, when a dream catcher was explained, Avril came up with the idea that she might catch her happy dreams by writing them down in a diary.

We often find that clients have considerable creative capacity in their solution-finding when given encouragement to explore how their existing talents can best be used. This increases our stock of potentially useful ideas to profer tentatively; clients' own solutions are always more effective than anything we could suggest as experts. And we must remember that if our 'expert' prescriptions are taken up and then fail to work, we are further undermining the client's developing story. Avril's achievements were amplified by careful editing of the notes made in this session; separating the possible solutions to the two main aspects of her current problems: being allowed out socially and difficulty in getting off to sleep, see below:

SESSION NOTES

PROBLEM
The same, although sleeping is a bigger problem than eating at the moment. Some nights it takes her 1–2 hours to get off to sleep and occasionally she doesn't sleep at all. Avril doesn't have nightmares but she does get intrusive thoughts which stop her getting off to sleep.

EXCEPTIONS/PROGRESS

1   Avril has been eating absolutely everything – and in front of people.
2   Avril's mum has not been checking on how much she is eating and this takes some pressure off her.

3 When Avril does manage to fall asleep, she then has good-quality sleep. She also takes advantage of the school holidays to sleep-in next morning to make up for a bad night.

4 She has got to 60 on the happiness scale. Some days are better than others; Darren has noticed more good than bad days, and Avril feels much happier when she is out socially (like playing darts in the pub with Darren and her dad).

THOUGHTS ON SOLUTIONS

1 Avril did the eating in the same way as she approached school dinners. She just did it. She took it easy and waited until she was ready for it.

2 She has tried a number of sensible ways to improve her sleep. She goes to bed when she feels sleepy, then lies as quietly as she can. If this fails to work, she gets up to watch television to distract herself from intrusive thoughts.

3 Avril can get off to sleep when Darren sits on the side of her bed.

4 She has already started reorganising her bedroom to make it a safer and more sleepy environment. She is redecorating it (it is currently a bit Gothic with red and black). When it is finished it will be a bright, fresh purple and white. She is changing her furniture round but the lighting is okay as it is.

5 Having a bird in her bedroom would help.

HOMEWORK

1 Avril may try the 6–5–4–3–2–1 exercise for getting off to sleep. She might also study her biorhythms and fit her getting ready for sleep round these.

2 She had the brilliant idea of catching happy dreams in a diary. Judith thinks it might help to catch happy moments during the day too.

3 She will discuss fifteen-year-old responsibilities and rights with her mum to remind mum that Avril is ready to grow up (and grow the problem down) and can be trusted to go to the pub with Darren.

Shane's answer to the 'what's better?' question was much more muted than Avril's – not surprisingly in view of the violence in his life – but it was still possible to amplify small achievements. The following extract from notes taken during this session shows how his control over his life can be made clearer through the use of questions about minute detail and prompts which thicken his initial 'thin' answers:

Counsellor: What's better?

Shane: I've not been arguing as much.

Counsellor: How have you done arguing less?

Shane: I'm not there that often. Weekends I stay at my sister's . . . I haven't seen my dad this week. He's been working.

Counsellor: Have there been less arguments overall, smaller arguments, or both?

Shane: The arguments with my mum have been big ones but they've been less in numbers.

Counsellor: Good. How did you do less arguing?

Shane: By not letting it get to me . . . turning it away from me . . . not telling her to shut up. I always want to get the last word in.

Counsellor: How long have you been able to keep it from getting to you?

Shane: Depends on how I feel in a morning. It's getting longer now for me to bite.

Counsellor: How are you doing that?

Shane: I've had enough. I'm not bothered any more. Bothered about myself, not what she says . . . Just ignore it.

Counsellor: Like, it's her problem, not yours?

Shane: Yes, basically. I don't need no shit from people. I'm trying to get on with people . . . She'll pick a fight tonight. She always does.

Counsellor: Every night when you come home from work?

Shane: Basically, yes.

Having avoided unproductive narrative lines and stayed with exceptions, the counsellor then allows herself to get sidetracked into discussing Shane's relationship with his mother. It would have been better to follow the narrative line which was exploring what he did differently to take responsibility for his own behaviour (not others') and ask him how he did 'getting on with people'. Equally, the counsellor did not show sufficient curiosity about the two other exceptions he had mentioned: 'turning it away from me' and 'not telling her to shut up'. Even though they may be missed in the flow of the conversation, possibly productive narrative lines are always worth revisiting. Although opportunities to thicken an emerging counterplot were missed and family and community violence was discussed prematurely, fortunately it was possible to return to exception-finding at a later point in the session:

> *Counsellor*:   So, let's see. Lots of people in your life are affected by violence. Dad hits mum and . . .
> *Shane*:   Mum slaps Shane. Dad *smacks* Shane. And Shane don't hit nobody and will do eventually. *Dad* . . . Me sister hits her boyfriend, then he leathers her . . . see it in the streets on a night.
> *Counsellor*:   Is there police violence as well?
> *Shane*:   I've been proper ragged about by police. Shoes and socks off when they've been searching me. We just laugh at them when they've nothing to do but search us.
> *Counsellor*:   Any violence at work?
> *Shane*:   No . . . Wednesday, I was making some tapers up at work, did the drawing wrong and they all had to be done again. And Terry was taking the piss and I thought I was going to blow. But I didn't.
> *Counsellor*:   How did you do not blowing? [and back to amplifying small achievements].

In cases like Shane's where a more narrative approach is being taken because of the obvious influence of dominant narratives on the maintenance of the problem, this is highlighted in the notes. For example, Shane's notes include more on unique outcomes (the times he resisted the influence of the problem) as well as straightforward exceptions. Also his qualities as a person are reflected on rather than being asked if, 'he knew this about himself' when achievements are being validated. The homework has all been decided by Shane and the fine details were worked out in the session to remind him how he will do it:

SESSION NOTES

PROBLEM
The same, except that Shane knows that violence is in his life rather than just in him. It seems to be making everybody unhappy.

EXCEPTIONS/PROGRESS

1   Shane has not had as many arguments with his mum lately.
2   He has also had less arguments with his dad.
3   Shane felt like blowing up at work when Terry teased him but he didn't.

4   He has been awarded a certificate in welding and has spoken with his boss about going back to college. Shane is really serious about being a good worker.
5   He hasn't been in any fights with his mates recently.

THOUGHTS ON SOLUTIONS

1   Shane did less arguing with his mum by not letting it get to him, turning away from it, and not telling her to shut up. He has also kept out of arguments by staying at his sister's house. He is confident that he can avoid an argument tonight by talking quietly with his mum.
2   He has done less arguing with his dad by talking to him only when he has to and keeping out of the way.
3   Shane managed not to blow up at work by remembering that he loves his job and wants to keep it. He can stick at things, even with all the upset in his life. This says a lot about Shane as a person.
4   Shane has a good understanding of how he is tempted to do violence. He has worked out that even though he can lose his temper any time someone says something to him, the worst time is when he has been drinking (not when he has had vodka as he can't do anything then). He can't stand people laughing at him or saying things. In the past, when he has tried to walk away from this or ignore it, ideas of violence have worked on his mates and when they wind him into the ground, he ends up fighting them. He knows that resisting invitations to violence when out with his mates is the first place he will make a stand against them.
5   Shane realises that other people in his life are fed up with the way doing violence is pushing them around and making life miserable. His mates have had enough and his sister and her boyfriend are considering counselling. It might just be that these people can form an alliance to stand with Shane against violence.
6   Judith feels optimistic about Shane as he has a clear idea about the sort of father and worker he wants to be. He knows how he will handle his kids when they do wrong without using violence. Shane has a really caring and considerate side to his nature (even if violence in his life keeps it out of sight a lot of the time).

HOMEWORK

1 Shane's mates are there for him emotionally as well as fighting so he will make a start on standing up to temptations to do violence when he is out with his mates. If anyone gets in his face, he will ignore it, refuse the wind up. He might also laugh at them but will remember to tell his mates to leave it too so that they don't wind him up.

2 He will discuss counselling with his sister and her boyfriend. Even if they decide they don't want counselling, they may still stand with Shane against the violence in their lives.

3 He will talk quietly with his mum about his plans and how to do arguing less even more.

When things are the same

While many clients report some aspects of life that are better, an equal number come in with long faces and say, 'absolutely nothing', or look puzzled and say that they don't know. In these instances it is best to begin again in much the same way as you would for a first session, although there are a number of questions which we find particularly helpful in getting solution talk going again. Since there can have been no void – something always happens – we are curious about the client's report that nothing has changed and listen to the current problem story, searching for tiny exceptions. We may ask clients to tell us about the day after the last session and the next day and so on. This often uncovers some changes that have been forgotten or discounted. For example, 'so tell me about yesterday', and then look for small times during that day when the problem was not quite as acute; what the client was doing differently at these times; and can they do more of it. If the client persists in saying that nothing is better at all, the counsellor can ask how they managed not to let things get worse, how have they endured all this without losing hope, or managing not to go backwards. Recognising how they did this leads to identification of skills and strengths which can then be used to get some forward momentum.

Alternatively the counsellor can do being puzzled, patiently waiting for an exception to emerge. For example, Janey's first session had explored her out-of-control behaviour when drinking with friends and the counsellor had been hopeful that Janey's own ideas for handling this would have led to increased success. Janey made her feelings plain at the second session by sitting down with a loud sigh and a bump, responding to the 'what's better?' question with, 'Absolutely nothing. Nothing *at all*. I've just been plodding on. That's all you can do, isn't it? Plod on.' The counsellor could have asked how she did 'plodding on', as this can be important for identifying endurance, but decided instead to opt for being puzzled:

Counsellor: Absolutely everything has been exactly the same? Every little thing?

Janey: Just plodding on. Just being bonkers like last time I saw you. Still like mad . . . but not as stupid as last time.

Counsellor: In what way have you not been as stupid?

Janey: I've not been kicking windows in, doors . . . Not losing control. I did a tiny bit on Friday but I didn't lose control. There was a reason for it. I was on a work night out and I didn't know anyone right well so I got drunk 'cos there was nothing else to do.

Counsellor: But you didn't lose control? How did you do that?

Janey: It was a different kind of drunkenness really. I was with people who would have thought it odd of me to behave mad when I'm supposed to be respectable.

Counsellor: So, you made a choice?

Janey: Yes. In a way . . . I couldn't act like that in front of people I worked with. I still got drunk, just didn't turn into a nutter. I'd gone with a friend who knew everybody and she was talking to them. I thought, this is going to be a bit boring, so I got drunk.

Counsellor: Are you proud of yourself for not turning into a nutter?

Janey: Don't know . . . It was horrible when I went bonkers that time. I got a terrible feeling, a gut feeling. I didn't get that this time. I just got drunk.

Counsellor: What did you do different?

Janey: I wasn't in the mood to go silly. I'd been in contact with the police all week [making a statement about a previous sexual assault] and I was quite down. Couldn't stop thinking about it. Tried to be daft but I couldn't.

This turned out to be a much more productive narrative line which enabled the counsellor to begin to start understanding her experience better; how her out-of-control behaviour when drinking was linked with her out-of-control experiences when assaulted and how she could separate these in her solutions. She hadn't been able to talk about this at the first session and it was important for the counsellor to thank the client for helping her understand her better. Formulaic though the exception questions may appear, we find that clients do not get at all irritated with our constant questions about 'how they did that', making serious attempts to answer. Similarly focusing on behaviour rather than emotions does not prevent them from saying how they felt; indeed they are able to talk about their emotions when they deem this relevant and are not in danger of being overwhelmed or exhausted by them. Clients who have previously experienced other forms of counselling often tell us that they prefer this pain-free approach to one which leaves them distressed for days after a session reliving all their most painful emotions.

When this approach fails to yield anything useable in the way of exceptions, we may check out the goal again, or we may counter pessimism with more pessimism. For example, the miracle question can be asked as a nightmare scenario (Berg and Reuss, 1998) or we ask what Dolan (1998) refers to as 'the pessimistic question': 'all problems have advantages as well as disadvantages. How can you keep the advantages but still get rid of the problem?' This is a very useful question as it encourages honest responses about the complexity of problems and their influence on people's lives. For example, clients' problems can seem like old friends in that a label excuses them from some responsibilities which they are not yet ready to take on, or are unsure how to resume. Equally, they can protect the client from further failure. For example, Ruth replied to the pessimistic question by saying that it gave her an excuse for not trying anything new. Simply hearing herself give this answer was 'sufficient for her to make a choice not to be dominated in the same way by the problem although, where necessary, the counsellor can follow up with a question asking if it still suits the client to be influenced in this way. With young children, this is often phrased in a way which encourages externalisation; for example, 'maybe [chosen name for the problem] has been in your life for so long it hasn't spotted that you have been doing some growing up? Maybe it doesn't want you to know just how much growing up you have been doing. Now that you are [age], are you still prepared to listen to this line of excuses [chosen name of problem] is feeding you?'

When clients genuinely don't seem to know what is better or what they are doing differently, we find it helps to join them in their 'not knowing'. Not only is it important not to be pushed into the role of expert, it is also essential to counter hopelessness by conveying a confidence that the answer is there, if only they can search deep enough. For example, when 13-year-old Ricky reported a slip back in his progress towards his goal ('I want people to say "he's a good boy"') and could not recall how he had managed the earlier improvement, saying, 'I really don't know how I did it. I only wish I did', the counsellor replied, 'so do I. Whatever can it be?' Ricky then returned to talking about how he had made a start on 'being good' in previous weeks, a counterplot which was particularly underdeveloped in his life; although he was an expert on 'being bad'.

If this approach fails to yield any useful narrative line, then the counsellor returns to searching for competencies away from the problem – however tangential. These are written down, with a comment to the effect that we are not sure how they will be used but they are bound to come in useful at some time. This validates the person apart from the problem, encourages hope that a solution will eventually be found, and broadens the scope for client creativity in solution-finding. For example, Robin viewed the teacher whose lessons most fuelled his temper as a roaring tiger and his father as a grumbling elephant sitting in an armchair eating peanuts. He enjoyed reading Harry Potter books and, despite being slightly built and asthmatic, identified with the character of Hagrid (the teacher in the 'care of wild animals'), so his potential talent in animal training was encouraged and his successful methods noted. His family and school problems were quickly solved by his application of gentle and encouraging 'animal training'. His misery over persistent wet beds (he referred to this problem as Friend Spoiler as he couldn't have friends in his bedroom because of a lingering smell of urine), was tackled by asking him what sort of creature Friend Spoiler was like and what sort of training it needed.

And, of course, there is always the basic suggestion of this approach, which is to do something different, anything. In those rare instances where nothing better can be identified, we do not ascribe this to client resistance, rather we apologise for not being more helpful and suggest that perhaps we start again; asking for permission to explore some crazy ideas. This can take the form of a formal restart; asking the client to go outside the consulting room and beginning again as though there had been nothing happening previously – this is particularly useful with young people as it gives them the opportunity to back down from an earlier position of hopelessness, injustice or lack of control over their own lives without losing face – or it can involve wide-ranging brainstorms. Brainstorms can be fun and, as any idea is listed – however unacceptable when the items are evaluated – it also allows the client to express antisocial solutions before moving on to 'doable' solutions. Alternatively, the client's wildest dreams can be explored. Usually they start these enthusiastically and then stop, saying that the dream is unlikely to come true. The counsellor can counter this by saying that it won't if a start is not made. However extravagant the dream, the first step towards it will usually contain the seeds of a solution to the more pressing problem. For example, 11-year-old Liam's dream was that he was world leader and everyone was cheering him. When asked what he was doing that made his people cheer, he said that it was because they loved him for his kindness. His first step towards his goal was, then, to begin being kind, and Liam thought the easiest place to start would be by being kind to his pets. It was then agreed that his family would cheer every time he fed his rabbits properly, instead of putting them on the lawn, and cleaned out his birds.

When things are worse

When clients report deterioration they are often very pessimistic, having experienced multiple disappointments and perhaps failed treatments. They frequently have several problems, each making the other worse, and they are often heavily oppressed in many areas of their lives. In these situations counsellors need to be cautious about expressing their own optimism – rather they need to emphasise that it will be very hard work. It is vital to listen more and cooperate with their feelings of hopelessness. This is helped by clearly getting into the 'not knowing' mode and checking out once more what they see as their 'real' problem and their preferred goal. They need more space to express their views, especially about the process and about past counselling experiences. As mentioned above, it often helps to switch into Dolan's 'pessimistic questioning', asking how do they manage to keep going in spite of all this, how come they have not given up before now, and when things do begin to get better what might be the first small hint of improvement? Also as 'veterans' of counselling, what do they think the *counsellor* could do differently or better.

Selekman (1997) sometimes asks such clients to predict what they think the next crisis will be, when, and where it will happen. It may be possible to plan jointly to counter such an event. Brainstorming past unrelated successes may help to utilise effective tools from other experiences. Selekman recommends tasks that disrupt patterns that maintain the problem – old failed solutions – and visualisation techniques, such as picturing the family at peace before going to sleep. When her assisted-lodgings placement broke down, Eva was returned to her parents by social services and came back to counselling saying that, although she was no longer self-harming and was holding down her job, her misery was worse. She was responding to her parents' emotional abuse by going to her bedroom to weep or spending her hard-earned wages at the pub, thereby setting back her plans to become self-supporting and independent. She felt that her future was completely hopeless, but harnessing her creative writing skills in the construction of an escape plan from her terrible situation sustained her through a difficult period, gave her something different to do from weeping in her bedroom and added considerably to her savings by keeping her out of the pub. The 'escape plan' was both a vivid and moving piece of writing and also an account of how she 'did' her solution.

When things are mixed

Our experience is that many clients respond to the, 'what's better?' question with comments such as, 'things are a *bit* better' or, 'not a lot', although this usually turns out to be significant change which has been discounted because it doesn't seem large enough to the client. Asking detailed questions about the small changes tends to increase their significance for these clients; especially when accompanied with an explanation of the snowball effect. However, sometimes people return to subsequent sessions with anxiety and concerns about their failure to make more progress. We normalise these concerns, often explaining that progress can be like three steps forward and one step backwards, underlining the value of small changes and the need to consolidate them. Asking suppositional questions about *when* there is further progress can help. These clients may need space to express possible concerns that we have not taken them seriously enough and we may need to check that we have not been rushing ahead of them. We may also need to consider whether they are customers for other, or different goals, as well as seeking out their unique ways of cooperating.

Prediction tasks help where progress appears random or not recognisably the direct result of their efforts. For example, Gary's planned move to an open prison with drug-counselling facilities broke down due to bureaucratic blunders, and his subsequent transfer to another closed prison further away from his family led to a major slip back. After having successfully resisted heroin use and staying out of trouble the previous six months, he smoked heroin offered by his cell mate, lost his job, and got into a fight within two weeks of his stay in the new prison. This entailed a loss of his 'enhancement' and his relationships with prison officers deteriorated. Although his parents maintained their newly-discovered faith in him, Gary was in despair at a prison system he perceived as unfair and uncontrollable. His justifiable sense of injustice obscured the small amount of control he still had over his situation so he was given a calender and asked to predict on which days he was likely to get on better with the prison officers. Analysis of his successful predictions enabled him to work out what he was doing that worked, where he could exert control over his future, and renewed his confidence in his ability to overcome the setback.

Listening to problem talk can sometimes move the goalposts. This is most likely to happen where a young person is complained about by a parent. For example, Sally and her mother had initially sought counselling for Sally's persistent fighting with her older brother, verbal abusiveness when asked to undertake household chores, and poor standards of personal hygiene. Sally's problem was externalised as a grumpy, growly, gobby bear (GGGB) and she made excellent progress in getting GGGB out of her life. On arrival for her third appointment, both Sally and her mum were sitting in the hall on adjacent chairs but their body language demonstrated a wide gulf. Mum entered the consulting room with a tight expression on her face and burst into tears as soon as she sat down, telling a long story about a huge row they had had the day previously. This was listened to and mum's feelings were acknowledged but the counsellor did not dwell on the reasons for it or suggest possible solutions, instead she asked about progress on the previously agreed goals. Sally had been successful in most items on her homework list: she had been polite to her stepdad, made her own bed, made her own tea when asked, had been bathing and washing her hair regularly, getting up in a morning without fuss about half the time, doing her homework before going out to play, not swearing (apart from the one row), and having less rows with her brother. They then identified how Sally had done all this: by a mixture of self-calming techniques on both their parts. When Sally began 'mouthing off', being 'gobby', mum would ask her in rap to leave the room for five minutes and then return when both of them had calmed down. This technique had been negotiated at the previous session to utilise Sally's sense of fun and mum's singing and poetry skills. As the 'how Sally did it' conversation continued, mum suddenly realised that she had not done *her* self-calming during the row as they had been outside at the time and she had been both tired and terribly conscious of neighbours overhearing. 'It was only the *one* row, even if it was a big one', she said, 'but I think we can work out how to get rid of GGGB for good on our camping holiday next week. I was dreading that but now I know what I'm going to do'. Sally, much relieved that her efforts to improve her good behaviour had been acknowledged, changed from the surly girl who had entered the room and joined in her mum's plans for getting GGGB out her life for ever. She thought she would throw GGGB over the cliffs on holiday. Six weeks later, at her next – and final – appointment, she announced that GGGB had floated away down a stream, adding, 'I thought I didn't want to grow up, but it happened anyway.'

When the process seems to be stuck

When the work feels stuck it is not unusual for the counsellor (or the supervisor) to sense that they are going too fast, which usually means they are pursuing their version of the goals rather than the client's specific version. Getting back to the day after the miracle, describing it in more detail and describing how the clients and others will be different is sometimes needed. Using scaled questions about various aspects of functioning can help to clarify matters further, and checking that what people first say they want is what they want. This slows the pace and checks worker ambition. It may also be necessary to check if the counsellor is working too hard at proposing specific solutions. Since it is extremely difficult to get this right, when we catch ourselves working too hard or proposing too many of our ideas to people, we find it is helpful to become *more vague*. This mobilises the client's expertise; for example, by suggesting that a person, 'take some steps in the direction that is good for him' (Berg and Miller, 1992: 201)

In relation to this, stuckness is often due to the goal being expressed as the *absence* of something, such as unhappiness. Many clients have difficulty in describing what they will have *instead* – they are unable to picture happiness and so the goal risks being a void which, unknown, can be worse than the problem. For example, Fiona went through a period of saying that things were both better and worse because she feared that she wouldn't be interesting once she had solved her problems. She could not yet envisage a problem-free future and worried that it would be blank and boring in comparison with her previous life – she had found the emotionally charged atmosphere of self-harming and 'being bad, being wild', exciting even though it frequently overwhelmed her. There were advantages also in her current experiences – she was making a statement about her father's earlier sexual abuse of her and felt 'like a star' when praised by the police officer taking the statement. Here questions focused on asking how she would know when she didn't need counselling any more helped to enrich her vision of a problem-free future; one that would involve a life of joy rather than heroic survival:

> People who embrace 'survivor' as their primary identity over the long term tend by necessity to filter daily living experiences through two criteria: how a current event resembles or differs from the traumatic thing that happened in the past, and how a current experience mitigates or worsens the continuing effects of past trauma. As a result, people who remain at the Survivor stage see life through the window of their Survivorhood rather than enjoying the more immediate and unconstricted vision of the world around them that they were originally born with. (Dolan, 1998: 3)

We need always to check for meanings. If 'happiness' has no meaning for a person it cannot be a useful goal unless there can be specific conversation about what the person will be *doing* that is different when they are happy; if that is a 10, where are they at now and what will they be doing when they are one step higher? Getting to 10 will not be easy, so what else will they need to do? Since life is not easy for any of us, how will they keep on their toes so as to get done the things they know they need to do?

Ending

Where clients express satisfaction with their progress, when the changes are good enough even if they are only changes of outlook, we compliment them on their success and reinforce this in their feed-back notes. In addition to the usual notes we may add specially designed certificates or diplomas. With children we celebrate the achievement by inviting the child's family to join them in an awards ceremony at which photographs are taken and a chocolate cake is shared. During the sharing of the cake, all members are asked to iden-tify how the success happened and what advice they can offer to other people with a similar problem; all this thickens the success story.

Summary

Unnecessary problem talk focuses on the past, is not 'progressive' and risks increasing stuckness. It is important, therefore, to switch to goals, exceptions and picturing or creating solutions in the future whenever clients become bogged down in problem talk in subsequent sessions. The work in these sessions entails eliciting any small improvements, amplifying these by discussing how the person did them and what difference they make, reinforcing changes by highlighting the difference between them and the old problem, 'making them more newsworthy on the meaning level of the client' (Selekman, 1997: 136), asking about any further changes – 'what else is better?', and discuss-ing how the progress can be maintained, or how the person can keep on-track towards their goal. If the tasks assigned in the previous ses-sion are working, the homework consists of repeating them. If not, they are asked to do something different.

6

Thoughts on personal relationships

Psychologising relationships

We begin this chapter by inviting you to answer two questions: how do you do happiness? and, what contributes to you having a sense of well-being? Please spend some time on your answers but do not discount any thoughts which pop quickly into your mind. If you find these questions difficult to answer, ask yourself how other people know when you are experiencing either state or remember the last time you were happy and what you were doing.

From the many responses we have heard to these questions, we would suspect that you are more likely to list items of personal achievement in answer to the first question, whilst replies to the second answer may include having love and support, but probably health and money too. Yet we can never be certain. We need to ask each client these questions and listen carefully to their answers if we are to find out what they will be like when they have met their goals.

If we had asked the questions in reverse, the answers might well have been different because misery and 'ill-being' have been studied more extensively and have, therefore, better developed narratives which may well have influenced your answers. You may have mentioned (wanting to be free of) any number of dysfunctional possibilities – low self-esteem, failure to maintain relationships, unresolved trauma, and so on. We argue that these various narratives are problematic because they locate unhappiness within the person, demanding particular ways in which to be and behave, and prescribing the ideal path towards the development of your 'true' self. At best, these narratives provide only partial explanations; for example, so-called low self-esteem is not a fixed trait, being usually context-specific (Jenkins, 1990: 54), relationships are influenced by class, race, gender and culture (Katz, 1996: 152), and the effects of trauma vary tremendously depending mainly on a person's degree of resilience and social support (Gilgun, 1999).

A significant narrative that we find particularly problematic is one of healthy relationship formation. We do not dispute that people are social beings and that they are happier and have a heightened sense of well-being when they are in supportive relationships. What we do take issue with is the way interpersonal relationships have become psychologised, preferred ways of maintaining relationships have been prescribed, and the mother–child relationship has been elevated to the primary relationship which underpins all others. For example, Bowlby says:

> attachment theory explains the differential development of resilient and mentally healthy personalities, and also of personalities prone to anxiety and depression, or to developing a *false self* or some other form of vulnerability to mental health. (1988: 132, our emphasis)

We consider this particularly important as counsellors' assumptions about 'healthy' relationship formation and 'true selves' are central to how they do counselling (the notion of a therapeutic relationship which reflects the mother–child relationship); what factors they select as significant in a client's story (mostly deficits); what they regard as a psychologically healthy end-state of counselling; and, how they 'interpret' client protests. A mother-therapist does not have to take her client-child protests at face value:

> should a patient react to an interruption by disparaging therapy or missing a session, a therapist who adopts attachment theory would ask himself why his patient is afraid to express his feelings openly and what his childhood experiences may have been to account for his distrust. (Bowlby, 1988: 153)

Although the research on which attachment theory is based studied mainly white, middle-class toddlers, it posits that where a mother reacts to her child in a loving, attentive and sensitively-paced way, the child is more likely to form a secure attachment to that mother. This basic, 'secure' attachment has implications for the later social encounters, the child being said to be more skillful in later years with peers and more curious and persistent in approaching new tasks – the notion of exploring from a secure base. Whilst not arguing against the process by which children form attachments, the extent to which this has been generalised from, in terms of essential emotional well-being and functioning, is worrying. Attachment theory has been invoked as an explanation for 'dysfunctional' behaviour at any stage of the lifespan; including adult bereavement (Bowlby and Parkes, 1970; Parkes, 1972), loneliness (Weiss, 1973), marital disharmony (Weiss, 1982, 1991), poor relationships between elderly parents and their children (Circirelli, 1989, 1991), dysfunctional family systems (Byng-Hall, 1985; Marvin and Stewart, 1990), families and depression (Radke-Yarrow *et al.*, 1985), child abuse (Crittenden, 1988), domestic violence (Bowlby, 1988), adult relationships generally (Feeney and Noller, 1996) and counsellor–client relationships (Kahn, 1997; Bowlby, 1988). This makes it appear to be an extremely useful theory for problem-focused counsellors; it not only clarifies both tasks and goals (if the client disagrees, they are said to be resistant or in denial or transference), but the counsellor does not have to listen to the client carefully and heed what is said. Neither does the counsellor have to be concerned about problems outside the consulting room, such as poverty (Bowlby's hypothetical client may have lacked the bus fare), inadequate housing, racism and so on, as attachment theory bundles up all problems within the person.

Attachment theory does not, however, generalise so neatly. For example, it ignores the fact that other people are significant in the lives of insecurely attached children; such as pre-school teachers (Bretherton, 1992), children of the same age and experience in children's homes (Horrocks and Milner, 1999), and adult partners (Harris, 1991). Having loving parents has *not* been found to be a pre-requisite for having a good marriage oneself (Wallerstein and Blakesee, 1996), so it is simply incorrect to presume that adults who are having difficulties in their interpersonal relationships are repeating earlier, unsatisfactory relationship patterns. Most significant is that attachment theory fails to consider gender differences in relationships. Why, for example, do children find it easier to forgive fathers for abusing them than mothers for failing to protect them (Holme, 2000) unless it is that attachment theory has supported a narrative about mothering which places such a heavy burden of perfection on women that they can never meet? It is so much easier to locate deficiencies in the least powerful individual, especially when that person can least resist being studied. Psychologists have researched women and children's behaviour much more extensively than men's behaviour.

An interactional lens on relationships

Attachment theory is basically a theory of love, characterised by commitment, intensity and sensitivity; but love is not simply a psychological state. It has many social facets, being but one pole of our constructions of the different sorts of relationships in which we engage. When we apply a social lens to interpersonal relationships, the notion of single, basic attachment becomes less significant. Weiss (1973), for example, identifies six different types of relationships throughout life; placing emotionally intense (love) relationships at the top of his list, followed by social friendships, and then those which have the capacity for nurturing, achievement and advice.

Not all relationships are, or need to be, of the same intensity, commitment or sensitivity. Whilst we would agree with Dolan (1998a) that a good, long couple relationship offers the greatest potential for joy, we would equally argue that that joy would be diminished if a couple lacked neighbours who would water their plants and feed their pets whilst they took a holiday. The relationship with these neighbours would need to be committed but not necessarily either sensitive or intense. Neither are intense relationships necessarily more satisfactory than less intense ones. For example, relationships which have a high potential for nurturing also have a high potential for conflict simply because of their intensity. Relationships which provide opportunities for the recognition of achievement are important components of how many people do happiness but are usually high on commitment and low on intensity.

The idea of 'commitment' is a relatively recent construction but it can place a heavy burden of expectation on people. For example, both Carol and Penny complained that their partners would not 'commit' themselves and, therefore, did not truly love them; a belief that was causing them deep distress:

> *Carol:* He comes from a stable background. I'm insecure. I feel I need him more than he needs me. He doesn't need me the same. He's like my dad. He'll tell me to do this . . . pick myself up. I depend on him too much. That's what other people tell me. I can't get it out of my head. It creates all sorts of problems. I'm not content. There's not many men who need women like women need men. That's not very feminist but I need him. I need to believe he loves me as much as I love him.

Penny: I've lost who I am. Lost my sense of humour. Don't know which direction to go in. Stuck in a void, can't get out. I did some counselling before, six weeks through my doctor and then another four. The counsellor said it was all down to feelings of rejection. I need to cope with that and not get rejected again.

As they both had histories of unsatisfactory relationships with their mothers (emotional abuse in the case of Carol and gross neglect leading to a Care Order in Penny's case), they could have been 'diagnosed' as suffering from anxious attachments and have their earlier relationships explored in counselling. Instead the counsellor asked them what their partners would be *doing* if they were confident that their partners loved them. Carol said that she could tell if someone loved her as he would never lie, give her lots of affection, say it at times when it's needed, do things for her, not cheat on her, and have a bond. Penny's list was slightly different; he would listen, be good in bed, give her lots of cuddles, and tell her he loved her. Their partners scored full marks on all their criteria other than *saying* they loved them, so the counsellor pointed out that they were *doing* love. Penny and Carol then remembered that their partners had *written* that they loved them on birthday and Christmas cards. Once they freed themselves from a story of spoken commitment, their anxieties disappeared. Conversely, when Sandy's violent husband begged her to return to him, she complained: 'He says he loves me. I wouldn't call what he did to me love!'.

And relationships are also context-specific. It can be a bad idea to have a secure attachment style if one lives in a community with a high turnover of residents, such as a children's home or a war-torn country, as this lays the person open to the risk of multiple bereavements. Neither is it necessary to become attached to one's counsellor; assistance can be provided in a warm, sensitive and approving manner without this needing to replicate clients' relationships with their mothers.

What is interesting to us is how clients frame their concerns. We find that women are most likely to seek help for difficulties in their interpersonal relationships, and men for lack of achievement or if their partners are threatening to leave them unless they change. The differences in how they present for counselling are constructed by problematic narratives which tell them what sort of persons they ought to be. We will examine these in turn and show how problem narratives can be addressed through solution talk and how the counsellor can shift the emphasis to accommodate different relationships between men and women.

Women's concerns

Women who come to counselling are much more likely than men to have internalised their problems; are more devastated by the destruction of relationships and loss of self-esteem; have a sense of lack of control over their lives; tend to blame themselves; and take responsibility beyond what is reasonable and realistic (see, for example, Berg and Reuss, 1998; Milner, 2001). Thus they tend to tell a failure-saturated story filled with self-blame questions, such as, 'I want to know why he needed to hit me'; 'why me, why did he abuse me?'; 'I ask myself, where did I go wrong?' These stories are embedded in a caring narrative; one that prescribes what 'being a woman' should be like; that expects women to be all nurturing, sensitive, empathic and emotionally expressive.

Regarding women as responsible for the emotional tone of the whole family, partly as a result of good mothering narratives which link them to their children by viewing them as central in providing the correct sort of care that leads to healthy physical and psychological growth, actually places them in a position of powerless responsibility (Rich, 1977) and encourages scrutiny of the performance of their role (Milner, 1993). Locating their competence as wives and mothers in their ability to deliver the right sort of psychological care ignores the social fact that their resources for the task are frequently overstretched and inadequate. Women often have restricted access to education, housing, and finance which means that they are often attempting to be sensitive and nurturing in conditions of considerable adversity; lacking both formal and informal support networks (such as nursery provision, leisure facilities), and living in an environment which is difficult if not downright dangerous (poor transport, unlit streets, broken lifts and so on). Many of the women we meet in counselling tell stories of self-blame for their perceived deficiencies, of suppressing their own wants and failing to care for themselves. Letham (1994) stresses the importance of recognising the accomplishments of women which may seem modest unless account is taken of the adverse circumstances in which they have occurred and the need to clarify what is, and what is not, within her control.

For example, Claire originally sought counselling for crippling panic attacks which started when she heard that she would be required to give evidence in court against her ex-husband who had raped and attempted to strangle her; and which revived memories of her father's earlier sexual abuse of her. She returned to counselling some months later, saying that she was 75 per cent satisfied with her life (her ex-husband received a lengthy prison sentence, she had remarried and had a baby), but she was beginning to have panicky feelings again. Her expressed goal was to have more confidence and trust in herself as a mother and wife. She had internalised her problem ('I need to relax more'), and was concerned about her perceived failure to get on with her new mother-in-law ('I need to find out what I'm doing wrong that makes her not like me').

Rather than join her in this psychologised story of emotional responsibility-taking, the counsellor looked for competencies away from the problem and exceptions to the panicky feelings. Claire reported that she was relaxed and cheerful at work and when she was alone with the new baby and her older daughter. The panicky feelings only occurred when she was tired or when her mother-in-law criticised her care of the children. Emphasising her achievements enabled Claire to recognise the pressures under which she was attempting to 'do' mothering; she had returned to a physically demanding job only three months after the birth of the new baby, who was looked after in her own home by her mother-in-law. This meant that she had to clean the house even when tired so that it would pass the stringent standards of her new mother-in-law.

Looking pleased at the acknowledgment of her achievements, Claire added thoughtfully that she would like to be able to stand up to her mother-in-law. This could easily have been a cue to launch into assertion training but this, too, is no more than yet another problematic narrative for women – locating yet more deficiencies in personal functioning – so exceptions to not standing up for herself were explored. Claire had stood up to her mother-in-law when she had criticised how she dressed the older child and she felt more confident when her hair was done. Acknowledging these modest achievements revealed that her assertion goal was also modest; like many women, Claire only wished to make sufficient changes to 'get by' without too much distress. The main change she wanted to make to her life was to ask her mother-in-law to do a few simple tasks in the house while she minded the baby. This was achieved through a coin-toss experiment – Claire would toss the coin she had kept from earlier sessions (again reminding her of her success in overcoming her panic attacks). If it came up heads, she would pretend that she was confident enough to give her mother-in-law a list of things to do while she was at work. If it came up tails, she would have an ordinary day. Only the one session was necessary for Claire to increase the amount of support she needed to fulfill her roles to her own satisfaction and for the panicky feelings to disappear.

Janice sought help for 'depression' which was characterised by constant tearful episodes and hopelessness about the future. She said that she was not coping with the children, two of whom were exhibiting behaviour disturbances and all were fussy eaters. It was hardly surprising that Janice had no sense of control over her life as she was caring for her own three children, her recently deceased brother's two teenagers, and, at weekends, her partner's two toddlers from a previous relationship whilst holding down a part-time job. On top of all this responsibility she was also being assessed by social services following her application to be made official foster parent to her brother's children. The scrutiny of social services was an extra burden, especially as they were recommending that she give up her part-time job to concentrate on the children. This would not only reduce her income but also remove the one situation where she could forget her worries and be reminded of her strengths.

The counsellor acknowledged her achievements and then asked her who came first in her family; getting her to rank every member. Like most mothers, Janice placed the children first, her partner second, then other relatives, and finally the family pets. The counsellor asked her where she came in all this (at the bottom), and suggested that she couldn't care for her family if she didn't care for herself too. Janice thought it wrong to put herself higher than her family, but the counsellor said that even if she came last that didn't mean that she had to be at the very bottom of everyone's list – on the doormat. Janice picked up the metaphor, commenting that everyone wiped their feet on her. To get herself up a tiny bit from the bottom, she thought that the children could help more and this led to identifying their abilities and strengths – the eldest, although the most disturbed, was good with the other children; the next one was good at washing up; the eldest girl was good at making people laugh; and so on. Janice's homework task consisted of utilising all these competencies to lessen the burden on her and she reported triumphantly at the next session that she was no longer a doormat: 'I'm at kitchen-sink level now'. We find 'moving up from the bottom' and 'asking others for help' most useful in working with all women who accept unreasonable amounts of responsibility and find them satisfied and hugely relieved with only a small step up from the 'bottom' – they rarely desire to 'be selfish' or overassertive and we guard against our own militant feminist narrative which would demand much more.

Another way of coping with self-blame and overacceptance of responsibility is to give women a checklist as a means of having a moratorium on guilt, an idea from Freeman *et al.* (1997: 77/8). The items on the list are potentially endless but each one needs to be paired with its opposite; see the following example of one we sent to a mother who attended counselling with her daughter:

Lots of parents blame themselves when their children have difficulty in eating and accuse themselves of all sorts of things. Please read the following list and see if you have been accusing yourself of any of these things. Also add if there are things you have accused yourself of which are not on the list. We are also interested in the self-accusations you have managed to avoid, and how, as this will help identify all the things you know you have been doing right:

- Have you accused yourself of having a child too soon?
- Have you accused yourself of having a child too late?
- Have you accused yourself of being too close to your child?
- Have you accused yourself of not being close enough to your child?
- Have you accused yourself of contributing to her difficulty in eating through not taking action early enough?
- Have you accused yourself of contributing to her difficulty in eating by taking action too soon?
- Have you accused yourself of going back to paid work too early or working long hours?
- Have you accused yourself of spending too much time with your child?
- Have you accused yourself of not being united enough as a couple?
- Have you accused yourself of being too united as a couple?
- Have you accused yourself of neglecting other members of your family because of concentrating on her difficulty in eating?
- Have you accused yourself of spending too much time worrying about other members of your family?

This mother, and her husband, were reassured that they had taken all reasonable action and were able to join in a discussion about what sort of responsibility they could *realistically* take for their daughter's difficulty in eating. Force-feeding in hospital had greatly distressed and angered her but they appreciated that the sight of their painfully thin daughter made them attempt to assume responsibility for her eating. At the subsequent session, this mother reported that she had worked away from home one night despite her daughter's threat to 'not eat' if she did so: 'I decided that the monster [the agreed name for the problem] wasn't going to push me around too.' She had gained the confidence to avoid taking unrealistic responsibility for her daughter's eating difficulties without seeming to reject her. Changing her relationship with the problem was helpful in encouraging her daughter to take reasonable responsibility for her own eating (a responsibility only she could take).

A further way of reducing guilt and self-blame is always to acknowledge what parents are doing right. This does not necessarily need to be explicit in detail; simply list all the good things you have noticed about the child and add something like, 'there is such a lot to be proud of, you must have been doing something very right'. This is a huge relief to parents who bring their children for counselling whilst expecting criticism of their parenting. Parents are so scrutinised and criticised, from the official surveillance of health visitors to the informal comments of friends and acquaintances, that we would like to extend an invitation to you to join our 'anti tut tut' club. This simply involves not 'tut tutting' at parents of screaming kids in public places. Instead you could volunteer praise every time you see children being well-behaved.

Men's misery

The men's stories we most commonly hear are often the converse of women's stories. They too are devastated by the destruction of relationships and lack of self-esteem but they tend to feel that they are not cared for enough, that their efforts are not appreciated. This is not surprising because 'being a man' in our society is in many ways the opposite of 'being a woman'. Rather than being nurturing and emotionally expressive, men are expected to be calm and cool, take the lead, solve problems in a rational way, and be a success *outside* the family. The economic power of men over women gives them an exaggerated sense of entitlement and status in relation to women and children and the storying of mothers as central to the healthy psychological development of their children allows men to rely on women to take the socio-emotional responsibility for all family members (for a fuller discussion, see Jenkins, 1990). The expectations that women will provide a secure base affects not only how counsellors tradition-ally interpret men's behaviour, but many men have internalised this dominant narrative. For example, when Alex found himself about to appear in court following yet another assault on his partner, he sought counselling for help with his failed relationship with his mother:

> Alex: My anger is about struggling to get where I am. I have no father to turn to, my mum wouldn't tell me who my dad was. It's affected all my relationships, I paid a price. A loving family is 'it' to me, all I ever wanted for my kids. Got married, raised my fists. I need to get it out. If something goes wrong, I put it on my girlfriend . . . smacked her for being late. I build up an argument, if she doesn't tell me what I want, I hit her . . . I only hit when I'm in a partnership. When I devote all my love to them and build a castle and it doesn't go my way, I get annoyed. I only hit her three, four times. Only occasionally. But it's bad when it comes . . . black eyes, split lips, fractured her jaw once. It's about attention. The attention I give them they should give it back . . . I first noticed it at eighteen . . . just anger at my mum for not telling me what I want to know about my dad . . . for leaving me with my grandma in Antigua. When I can get this anger out, talk about it more, then I'll be able to walk away from it.

Thus Alex has entered himself in a psychological story which explains his violent behaviour as a product of his unsatisfactory early relation-ships. The counsellor could join with him in this story and explore his feelings of rejection or she might have a dominant narrative of her own – challenging men's violence being a popular therapeutic story (see, for example, Dobash *et al.*, 1996). Exploring internalised narra-tives by asking Alex how he did 'being a man' revealed that although he had only raised his fists to his female partners he was aggressive over a range of situations. He worked as a driver and was intolerant of other road users, swearing when frustrated and using the size of his vehicle to intimidate; frequently crashed the telephone back on its cradle when he didn't get his own way in conversations with officials; and was generally tense, angry and friendless. His conversation was saturated with masculine metaphors of individual control and the need to 'be someone' powerful and successful outside, as well as inside, the home. Denborough (1996) argues that the central importance of dominating and controlling others underpins a theme of masculinity that makes it harder for men to develop alternate ways of 'being a man'. Thus it is important to externalise internalised narratives about masculinity rather than simply search for exceptions to male violence. 'Being a man' is a problematic narrative for both men and women as it is practically impossible for any man to 'be a man' in all situations. It is not only women who feel the effects of male power; men may be powerful as a group but often feel individually powerless. Messerschmidt (2000) argues that, as masculinity is a social construct that reflects unique circumstances and relationships, different types of masculinity can exist simultaneously.

Challenging male violence or searching for exceptions to it merely tracks men along the well-worn lines of masculinity narratives. Denborough (1996), for example, suggests that it is much more useful to ask males what would be their preferred way of 'being themselves', inviting them to consider when they felt compassion, consideration and caring for others; that is, talking with them as we do with women. Elliot (1997) also criticises challenging men as this leads to counsellors focusing on increasing women's assertion skills (becoming more like men) and enters men into psychological stories which depend on women to police their behaviour and nurture them. She raises the issue of gender as a possible context for behaviour by asking questions such as, 'how as a father, as a man, do you handle these issues?', and suggests that it is more fruitful to increase men's *listening* skills. Alex, for example, did not need to 'get his anger out', or 'learn to walk away from it', after he had begun to listen to other people: 'I comforted her . . . made her feel safe and not pressured. I gave her choices, didn't say, "I want, do this, do that". She noticed, said I was less demanding than I used to be. I never did this before and it felt good.'

Entering someone into an oppositional masculinity story often has the effect of ignoring experiences of powerlessness. Marcus was referred for counselling by his Youth Offending Team for 'anger management'. He was described as an extremely violent young man given to racist attacks, and who was also about to be excluded from school for bullying. His large physical size and sporting prowess added to the picture of a dangerous young man but he talked about being a wimp in his early years at school when he was unable to cope with constant taunts about a large scar on his face and regular beatings from older, larger boys. Lacking a capacity to make an adequate verbal response due to his learning difficulties, he eventually began to hit back. His development of an oppositional masculinity at school then transferred to other threatening social situations – he responded to any perceived wind up with violence, resulting in a street fight being storied as a racial assault – and he began to take his temper home too, verbally bullying his younger brothers and sister. Although he could hold his own in most fights, he described living with temper as even more miserable than the early school years of taunting and physical abuse. He was able to identify several exceptions to his temper: he had never hit a girl, he didn't lose his temper when he had something physical to do, and he could sometimes walk away from trouble. However, in an exploration of what 'being himself' would be like, it was all about developing his more caring side. His preferred future was to be like an uncle who he described as tough but gentle. Borrowing from this life he admired was the way in which Marcus was able to 'be himself' with no anger in need of 'managing'.

Inviting men to take more responsibility for their behaviour and become more caring enables the counsellor to recognise men's vulnerability and misery whilst, at the same time, not providing them with excuses for their antisocial behaviour. Exploring what their preferred futures are like when they are 'being themselves' provides men with opportunities to be emotionally expressive. Carl referred himself after a huge weekend drinking binge to 'blank out' his relationship failures which ended with him recovering from an overdose in a hospital ward full of elderly, confused men. Carl's thoughts were not that these men were in a sad state but that he might not even live long enough to get old and confused. He introduced himself as 22 going on 12 and said that he had three problems:

Carl: Main one is the amount I go out and pour down my throat and then walk into a fight and think nothing of it. Or create one. Drunk or sober. Girlfriend is a big contributing factor. Home life and something recently which has to do with work . . . they all come on a par as I can get equally wound up about all three.

He had spent £350 on beer in the one weekend following his girlfriend telling him that he would not be able to see their expected baby if he didn't go back to her. At the same time problems with his flatmate had come to a head, he was about to lose his job, his mother wanted him to return home but he couldn't tolerate her nagging or get on with his stepfather, and he saw his violence as outside his control:

Carl: It's like a popular idea but I do see red. Round the outside
and the person I'm going for and that's all I see. One minute I
could see you normal but then I couldn't see behind you and
just see red and the part I'm aiming for. I hit. Draw blood. Seeing
blood doesn't bother me. I like them on the deck 'cos then I
know I've done it right. I also walk into gang fights . . . or create one. We were skating. I'm good at ice skating and we were
doing these turns. This lad got in my way and I ice sprayed him
as I turned. He effed and blinded and then one of his mates spat
in my face. I nodded to my best mate and we got a gang together,
went speed skating after them. I speed skated right up to him,
nutted him, jumped up and started kicking him with my blades
on. I didn't feel it at the time but I was cut to ribbons. Broken
knuckles, blood coming out of my ears, my legs slashed to pieces.
All my mates waded in. Then we had to have a police escort out
of the place, the others had rounded up a gang and were waiting
for us when we came out. I got a right buzz off it, I were laughing
halfway through . . . After, I think I wish I could go again, feel sort
of . . . smug satisfaction. It was a real high. I do a lot of stuff . . .
some I remember, some I have to be told. Usually by a copper
afterwards . . . My temper's like my real dad's. I don't remember
much, just him being violent.

There was no violence in his preferred future, explored through a 'back
to the future' scenario with prompts for detail, which was all about
being a caring father:

I'd be sat in a studio room with everything nice around me. Nice
plain room just how I want it. I can see the baby with me but
not Katie (his girlfriend). It's a room in a flat, I've always liked
flats. I'm buying it. Two bedrooms. Downstairs flat. No garden. I
hate gardening. The room's white, with a bit of red to show my
colours. Same throughout the flat, the floor's the same . . . pine,
or something pine-coloured. Definitely pine furniture. Baby's room
is full of things for it to play but not so full it'll get spoiled. A
lot of educational things. Picture of Katie in the room. I wouldn't
stop Katie from seeing the baby. Names of parents, grandparents,
best mate, work, baby's mum in the telephone book. And doctor . . . and hospital and things like that. I'm frightened of the baby
being poorly already. One dog . . . I'm fully trained for my job

so I earn serious money and I'd have . . . Katie's been on about returning to work after the baby, so I could pay for a child minder in the morning and Katie have him in the afternoon. Sometimes to stay overnight. [He is asked what his first small step will be.] Sit down and talk it out. Throw myself into work and learn as much as I can, earn as much as I can, and prepare for the baby. Also get out of the environment I'm in at the moment. Stay with mum, get on better with my stepdad. No more drinking . . . no fights. [He is asked what he can do instead when he sees red.] Breath deeply and think about the baby. Thinking about the baby helps. Main thing that comes into mind is the picture of the scan. I care for baby, big time, if no-one else. I carry this scan with me. I'm proud to show it. Think baby. Baby, baby, baby.

Focusing on developing 'being a caring, responsible father' instead of being a hard-fighting, hard-drinking man enabled Carl to begin listening to other people, show consideration, and negotiate improvements in his life. At the next session three weeks later he reported that he was 95 per cent in control of his temper. He had obtained a job at the same place as his stepfather and which provided learning opportunities, negotiated his way out of his flat share, improved his relationship with his mum, talked things through with Katie so that he could still be a responsible father to their child even though their relationship was over, cut down his drinking to two pints of beer on weekend nights, joined a rugby club (where his coach complimented him on not retaliating to a deliberate elbow in his face), resisted a wind-up socially, and been referred to by his best mate as a person who *used* to have a temper: 'I feel good about myself. I got into a lot of conversations with people . . . I don't feel as intimidated by educated people as I used to.'

Inviting men to develop the caring side of themselves can be done playfully too. After consulting young women about what they looked for in boyfriends, we devised a 'getting and keeping a girlfriend' chart (see Appendix 3e). We ask young men to rate themselves according to the categories and then decide which areas they want to work on improving. We also ask them to consult the women in their own lives and add to our list. One young man added his sister's criteria:

1   Be faithful and don't sleep around.
2   Not come home at all hours.

3   Don't come home drunk and make a scene in the sreet.
4   Don't expect all her money – just like my sister's ex-boyfriend.
    Nobhead!
5   Don't take drugs.

We find that men often do want to talk about how to negotiate and improve relationships. They rarely want children to prove their manhood; genuinely wishing to be more satisfactory fathers than their fathers have been for them – a persistent theme in our work with men is the lack of conversations between sons and fathers. Simply, they lack the experience and knowledge of how to be different. As a beginning to developing a way of 'being different', we also use the family differentiation exercises suggested by Dolan (1998a: 126).

Couples work

Solution-focused and narrative ideas are rapidly becoming popular in couples work. The process and the philosophy is the same as that with individuals. Goals are developed, life without the problem is talked of in detail, scaled questions are used, the problem can be externalised and exceptions, and how exactly they were done, are discussed. Hudson and O'Hanlon (1991) advocate getting beyond blame, invalidation and explanations since these do not help. They do not accept that partnerships are *determined* by the past, although they may be influenced by it. Neither do they see people as sociologically determined: 'The most changeable aspects of the couple's situation are each partner's actions and interpretations of the other's actions. We call this changing the "doing" and changing the "viewing" of the problem' (1991: 10). As in other work, people's feelings and inner experiences are validated, whether they are 'rational' or not. This is not just a 'reflecting back' ('so you feel angry'), but an explicit acceptance and acknowledgement of the validity of what is felt, without agreeing with it or taking sides. This is no easy task as individuals who are very upset will ask, 'wouldn't you be hurt?' and the counsellor needs to reply with something balanced like 'That would hurt me but I can also understand how her frustration could have led her to it'.

Also useful is using the distinction Hudson and O'Hanlon (1991) make between *facts* (what observers could see happening) and *experiences* (inner feelings and sensations). For example, Karen and Donna hoped to save their relationship despite Karen having smacked Donna after she admitted to an affair with a close friend of the couple. The counsellor commented that it seemed entirely understandable to her that Karen would *feel* anger but that it was not all right to *do* anger. Hudson and O'Hanlon also distinguish between *facts*, *experiences* and *stories* (the meanings and interpretations given to facts). Each person will have their version of events and points of view, interpretations and theories about events; and, in Karen's case, the storying of herself as a victim driven to violence was fuelled by comments from others: 'everyone I talked to about it, they agreed they'd have belted her one as well. It's not as though she ever does anything in the house. She just comes in from work and sits in front of the television.' So many conflicts are like 'duelling stories' but these stories are not usually neutral; they make most situations worse with a poisoning effect and the more they are narrated the more they take on the semblance of 'truth'. They may also include elements of mind-reading, prediction, labelling and generalisation. There is no way of telling which is the more true and therefore it is important not to enter into making judgements but to accept both sets of feelings while casting doubt on 'explanations' and considering alternative story lines; for example, changing 'sitting in front of the television' to 'tired – she's been working hard', to begin generating a story that supports the relationship and contains possibilities for change.

So while we do not try to change people's experience of problems, we do seek to change the story and the doing. Mutual tasks are developed, often including a 'pretend' which the other person has to try to spot. These pretend tasks allow people to change while staying the same; that is, they can experience change in a way that is playful and saves face. Tasks can interrupt old patterns and, because interactions are involved, even small changes made by one person can affect the behaviour of the other, setting off the possibility of a new pattern. Experimentation and even new rituals can be developed.

Communication is frequently mentioned as at the heart of relationship problems and people are therefore invited to not rely on mind-reading ('he should know what I need'), rather risk asking for what they want from each other. Likewise, identifying strengths and stories of overcoming problems in the past, or stories of what worked well in the past, is important. In some cases, however, it may be necessary to agree clear limits to certain behaviours that may be destructive or dangerous. Even though we avoid blame (attributing bad intention in past actions), we do expect that people are to be held accountable for future acts and we would challenge ideas of non-accountability and discuss consequences.

Separation or divorce

When a marriage or a partnership cannot continue for some reason, the process of separation holds much pain and difficulty for many couples in our culture. Sometimes there is relief but there is often a sense of loss and sometimes considerable grief, although it is difficult to say to what extent the process has been made painful by how it has been spoken of over many years. Do some people, for example, feel that they will be bad persons if they fail to fight bitterly? We cannot know why some let go easily and others, sometimes the victimised party, seem unable to let go.

Separation problems often involve battles over children and mixing up the parental role with the spouse role. People often need to be reminded that no-one is divorcing the children, that the parental partnership will go on, that only the spouse relationship is ending. Children can become third parties in a triangle, carrying messages and listening to stories of blame and denigration. Children can end with divided loyalties and much avoidable distress, even feeling they are to blame for the conflict. Keeping clear boundaries between marital discord and parental responsibilities is a great service to children and indeed may help some couples with their changing relationship; for example, if parenting regularly comes before partnering tension may result, or if parents do not act as a united team discipline problems can result.

The aim of divorce counselling is to help people avoid a 'bloody' divorce by staying out of the past, looking at the present and planning for the future. People can be helped to request future behaviours, such as communicating about the children, sharing assets and caring for the children's health and education, and they can be invited to reassure each other over concerns. The post-divorce relationship can be storied as a business partnership, the business being the rearing of the children, characterised by politeness, keeping to arrangements and being punctual at hand-overs, keeping a diary of plans, making telephone calls or writing notes for each other, and so on. Conflict can be externalised rather than analysed with alliances built against it.

Externalising conversations include such questions as, 'conflict has a grip on you – how did it get its claws into you so much? what is that doing to you? how can you begin to shake it off?'. We mediated with a couple who were intensely bitter, with high conflict dominating the meeting. To prevent matters escalating, we invited them to consider, since the process was 'going nowhere', to 'leave Conflict outside the door for the rest of the session – make it wait out there – it's stopping you from what you need to do'. They half-heartedly agreed to the suggestion and then we asked if they would agree to our pointing out to them if they began to 'invite Conflict back in'. During the remainder of the session, the discussion started to became heated on a few occasions and we did prompt them to 'keep the door closed on Conflict'. This helped them to make some useful progress.

Feelings of entitlement can be questioned as constructed by vested interests that restrain fairness. Trust can be constructed as not given but achieved. Winslade and Monk (2000) ask questions like: 'does this way of being suit you?', if not, 'what does this say about your attitude?, how determined are you to take action?, what hopes have you for dumping the conflict?, when it is dumped, how will you be talking about the children?, how long will it take to get good-will back?, what difference does this thinking make to both of you?'. As the couple in dispute begin to see each other as not the enemy, they become more able to move forward, seeing conflict as the mutual enemy.

Our thinking about the complexity of relationships, and the multiple influences on them, underpins some of the ideas in the three following chapters.

7

School and work

Traditionally, counsellors who view the mother–child relationship as the primary one regard school as the place where secondary, and therefore less significant, socialisation occurs as part of the child's development to adulthood and work. For example, Erikson's stage theory posits three 'parented' stages of early childhood as setting the direction towards 'the possible and the tangible which permits the dreams of early childhood to be attached to the goals of an active adult life' (Erikson, 1950: 230), with schools offering children an *economic* rather than an *emotional* ethos.

We view the school and work years as much more complex and fluid, with 'identity' being continuously reconstructed and re-evaluated, 'like a text being re-read or a story retold' (Katz, 1996: 52), with no notion of either 'true' or 'false' selves. Both school and work provide many opportunities for people to have different relationships from those they have in families, and more opportunities for achievement – indeed school has been shown to be pivotal for children in unsatisfactory home situations (for an overview, see Blyth and Milner, 1997). However, people in the social institutions of school and work are entered into stories which have potential to totalise and pathologise them. These stories are infinitely variable, depending largely on the political climate dictating the research and therapy. Thus, as previously mentioned, attachment theorists construct stories about truancy or school phobia in terms of troubled children's early relationships, whereas a more sociological perspective stories the same children as disaffected (teachers' fault for not making learning more relevant to pupils) or disruptive (the effects of peer group pressures and the development of anti-school attitudes). These stories fluctuate in where they locate the roots of the problem, with both psychological and sociological stories overlapping. For example, troubled and troublesome pupils are storied as both socially dangerous (in terms of youth crime when pupils are out of school in communities with increasingly ageing populations), and individually disturbed (dyslexia and hyperactivity being examples of the medicalisation of patterns of behaviour to explain in-school behaviour that troubles teachers). Workers' stories are rather less variable; they tend to be totalised as a group (threatening strike forces, for example) or individually psychologised as stressed or burnt out.

The people we see in counselling have usually been entered into one or more of these stories, none of which has the capacity to fully explain the client's distress since their difficulties are seldom single issues. Whilst it is possible to adopt a solution-focused approach to the resolution of school or work problems (see for example Kral, 1989; Molnar and Lindquist, 1989; Kowalski, 1990; Durrant, 1993), we also draw on narrative ideas which illuminate the oppressive potential of school and work to enter clients into stories (Freeman *et al.*, 1997). For example, 13-year-old Ryan was referred by his Youth Offending Team worker, who said of him:

> This young person has been dealt with in relation to a final warning programme. On speaking to him he stated that he saw his mother being beaten by ex-partners. He will not communicate to anyone how he feels but has become more and more aggressive towards his four younger brothers and sisters. In my opinion this young man needs help to overcome the past.

This was a story which substantially repeated his mother's analysis of the problem. After asking to see the counsellor separately from Ryan she said:

> Nine years ago I moved to Scotland to get away from his dad's violence. Ryan saved my life once; he got his dad off me by grabbing his goolies. It's witnessing all that violence that makes him so aggressive with his [younger, step] brothers and sisters. I've tried talking to him about it but he doesn't seem to have much memory of it, apart from that one time. It'll be hard getting him to talk; he's very withdrawn. If he can talk about it, all the violence he witnessed, then he'll get over it. If you can draw him out about it . . .

Ryan turned out to be a pleasant, chatty lad, who described his problem differently:

I don't want to be in no more trouble for fighting [at home and school] . . . I kick off when they tease me . . . I hit Simon when he calls me names, swear words . . . Samantha not as much. When she pulls faces at me. Graham when he says I don't have a proper dad . . . Beth's right nice. I play with her, 'cept when she wants to play Barbies!

After getting more detail about what happened when Ryan 'kicked off', the counsellor changed the grammar and introduced metaphors to develop an externalisation:

Ryan has been living with a temper for as long as he can remember. When he is wound up, his face goes red and he kicks off. It is like a ball of fire that gives him no warning at all. The fireball gets him to shout, kick, punch and stamp around. After the fireball has done the damage, it leaves Ryan feeling sad. The fireball lives in the bedroom mostly but recently it has started to push Ryan around at school getting him to fight with a bully.

These four descriptions say quite different things about Ryan and suggest different treatment strategies. There is 'narrative power' in each storying, although the reader may wish to consider which would be the least pathologising or the most constructive. The latter externalising version evokes some possibilities while avoiding imposing any judgement. We are interested in the problematic story that has developed and in 'the doing and the viewing' of events, as doing affects viewing and vice-versa. Constructionism considers how meaning is made and how problems develop when oppressive stories are 'performed' about selves and about relationships. Focusing on competencies can undermine such stories so that a new story can be co-created. Our interest is not in diagnosis but in drawing on the client's unique knowledge and abilities and ideas about the future:

The constructionist notion says that we act on a particular meaning (e.g. disinterested, apathetic student) as if it were the only truth about the problem, instead of merely one of several plausible meanings for the same event or behaviours (e.g. quiet, respectful observer). Since meanings are pragmatically selected based on the idiosyncratic aspects of the problem and people involved, the usefulness of specific interpretations (e.g. hyperactivity) will vary from case to case. (Murphy, 1992: 62)

By the time a problem has been brought to a counsellor it will have a variety of explanations attached, frequently associated with deficits or personality traits. These will seldom suggest a way forward so it is important to look elsewhere for change. Therefore we will set tasks to alter perceptions; for example, asking a teacher to note when a pupil is different:

> the behaviour of everyone in the classroom or school influences or is influenced by the problem behaviour . . . change in anyone associated with the problem has the potential to influence the problem behaviour. We believe this is a hopeful point of view because it says that everyone in a problem situation has the capacity to influence it positively. (Molnar and Lindquist, 1990: xiv)

When teachers make referrals, therefore, it is useful to ask them to do some observations to help the work. These can involve listing occasions when the pupil is different in some way. The pupil may be able to build on these different times but the observation process will have changed the teacher, sometimes by widening their view of the context; for example, when the child is better behaved if not sitting with friends. Kral has produced a Solution Identification Scale which was revised by Parton and O'Byrne (2000) as a Student Strengths Scale (see Appendix 3f), which enables pupils to rate various strengths and thereby realise their unnoticed abilities. These processes thicken the story, filling out areas that the problematic story has cut or ignored, opening the way to exception-finding.

As most of the schoolchildren we see are referred by their parents, teachers or school nurses, and adults are much more likely to self-refer, it is tempting to hypothesise that their problems are purely personal rather than seek to locate them within unequal power relations. Adults do not seem at first glance to experience the institution of work as oppressive as children do the institution of school. Adults do not complain so intensely about their managers as children do about individual teachers; rarely raise 'unfairness' as an issue; and have the capacity to change jobs if they are dissatisfied. In some instances their work problems are largely intertwined with problems in other areas of their lives. For example, men who are violent towards their partners almost invariably answer 'not at all' to the question 'I have ways of handling frustration at work' on the Overcoming Violence Scale (see Appendix 3d), and young men often struggle with their sense of masculine identity when they leave school for work.

It is our experience, however, that adults are also storied as deficient by their employers and have problematic perceptions of themselves; it is simply that these stories are less accessible because they are not written down on the referral form, and because they have been internalised over a lengthy period. The location of competence, of strengths and exceptions, is crucial to progress here too. Difficulties at school or work for which people seek help from counsellors are seldom simply due to a personal deficit. They are far more likely to involve interpersonal problems arising from oppression of some sort on the part of peers, teachers or managers, or to have a 'lack of confidence in achievement' element which gives rise to fears of attending school or work, or complaints about the work produced. These complexities are dealt with through the discipline of the solution-focused practice but also by being open to the creative possibilities of narrative work.

Taking age-appropriate responsibility

Freeman *et al.* (1997) introduce the notion of 'growing up and growing the problem down' in a playful way in their work with young children:

> Our aim is to access and collaborate with their imagination and knowledge . . . Instead of simply reflecting a child's language or listening and making theoretically based interpretations, we seek to be welcomed and active participants in the child's world of meaning. (Freeman *et al.*, 1997: 7)

We find this idea a useful way of approaching age-appropriate responsibility-taking at both work and school as we find that people of all ages have the capacity to generate solutions we would never have thought of, and enjoy being playful – as the work with Ryan illustrates.

Despite being described as 'this young man' on his referral form, Ryan was small and slight for his 13 years. Neither was he at all withdrawn, being only too keen to talk about how his stepbrothers and sisters 'wound him up'. Combined with his learning needs, these factors probably contributed more to his current aggressive behaviour as he may well have lacked the verbal skills to counteract hurtful teasing; and his 'withdrawn' behaviour may have been a response to the sadness he experienced after fighting. However, the counsellor did not need to explore any of these potential hypotheses about his 'deficits' as it was possible to identify many skills he possessed and utilise these in an invitation to grow up and grow the problem down. He had already done some self-calming by going to his bedroom to listen to music (it is much easier for people to do more self-calming than it is for them to stop doing temper). This had only been partially successful as he shared a bedroom with his oldest stepbrother, the one who wound him up the most. He had also begun a diary and chart for his 'good' days but no-one had noticed these. Homework for Ryan consisted of strengthening these existing solutions. Using a metaphor of fireball fighting, Ryan came up with the following plan:

1   He will put his fingers in his ears when Simon teases him. This way he can ignore him.
2   When Samantha pulls faces, he will shut his eyes.
3   When Graham makes comments about him not having a proper dad, he will cover his ears and smile.
4   He will count up to ten before he kicks off.

The counsellor added:

Ryan's parents will do some homework too. They will keep a diary of all the times they notice Ryan doing self-calming. At Ryan's next appointment, we will compare their diary with Ryan's plan.

At Ryan's second session three weeks later, he reported that he had only 'kicked off' a few times and none of these resulted in fights, although he had raised his hand level with Simon's face. His first attempts at ignoring Graham had resulted in more teasing so he had added singing 'la la la' to his repertoire of responses. His school behaviour had improved to such an extent that he earned more merits than any other pupil in the previous two weeks. Mum confirmed Ryan's success, saying that she had noticed how hard he was working to 'redirect his anger' and that she was supporting him by stopping the other children teasing him. Stepdad reported that Ryan had cleaned out a space in the cellar where he and Simon could play. The whole family being more interested in the solutions Ryan had discovered than the possible source of the problem, they accepted an invitation for Ryan to go in for his silver certificate in Thirteen-Year-Old Responsibility-Taking: another playful idea from Freeman *et al.* (1997) which is endlessly adaptable to individual circumstances, see the following details of the practice programme:

> Over the next three weeks, Ryan will:
>
> 1 Ignore his brothers and sisters when they wind him up by doing his self-calming — going to his bedroom to listen to music, putting his hands over his ears, closing his eyes, smiling, and singing la la la. He will do this most of the time.
> 2 He will not hit his brothers and sisters at all. He will do this by counting up to five and stopping his arm at three.
> 3 He will not hit anyone at school. He will do this by using his self-calming and telling his teacher if he gets bullied.
> 4 He will stay in school each day. He can do this by just deciding.
> 5 He wants to be even higher than 10 on the 'good behaviour at school' scale! He will make a start on this by working harder in his maths lesson.
>
> Ryan has chosen mum to be his trainer. Mum's trainer's job includes:
>
> 1 Making sure that Ryan is fit and well for the practice programme by giving him healthy meals and making sure he gets plenty of early nights.
> 2 Noticing when he does self-calming and telling him how he did it so he can do more of it.
> 3 Keeping good discipline (with dad) — like a football team trainer.
>
> At school, Ryan might ask one of his teachers to be a trainer too. The more people notice what he is doing well, the better.

The chosen means for each of Ryan's five tasks were developed with him, and mainly by him. Mum and stepdad worked out what they thought a trainer's job description would be. After a successful practice session to allow for any amendments necessary, a period of eight weeks was chosen for Ryan to complete the criteria for the silver certificate (a completely arbitrary category chosen by the young person on the basis of their confidence to solve the problem). On completion, he was presented with the certificate in a ceremony which includes photographs and a chocolate cake. Depending on whether amendments are needed or not, the whole process requires only four or five sessions.

Chrissie was referred by her employer after an unspecified crisis which, unusually, did not become any more clear when Chrissie attended her first session. She told the counsellor that she was having 'difficulties' at work and wanted 'to get things sorted out' before taking a sabbatical to travel abroad for a year. She hinted at some sort of breakdown at work but, apart from feeling unsupported by management and lacking organisational skills, she did not seem capable of giving further detail. The counsellor struggled with Chrissie's story which was rambling, with abrupt changes of topic and full of one-off statements, such as: 'I've been struggling with myself. I've come to a block. I'm rebelling against myself'. The counsellor deliberately became more puzzled as a means of helping her explain herself but this was not productive so a pretend task was suggested to help her get through her last few weeks at work: to borrow from a life she admired (a colleague she identified as having excellent organisational skills), and pretend to be that person on the days when the coin toss came up tails, having an ordinary day for comparison when the coin came up heads.

Writing up her notes proved difficult for the counsellor. After she had edited out all the questions and answers that did not lead to a useful narrative line, there was nothing left. There were words though, and these were used to construct a scenario with as much hope for the future as possible; see the following extracts from, first, the 'problem' section of the notes and, second, the 'thoughts on solutions' section:

At the moment Chrissie lacks confidence in her ability at work and home; this is affecting her health, motivation and thoughts – which tend to be negative. Chrissie has experienced a good deal of well-meant, but confidence sapping, criticism in her life. She is a sensitive person who does not shrug off criticism easily. Although she has no idea what she will be like in the future, she does know that she will be more balanced. Chrissie values peace more than ambition.

Chrissie is a very interesting person who can cope with her own company. She may just not be a management person – possibly more footloose and fancy free – and probably more creative and relaxed under these circumstances. Her coping strategies to date have focused more on what she is doing wrong and not enough on what she can do well and what she *wants* to do. This is bound to get in the way of being 'balanced'.

A fortnight later, Chrissie reported several successes at work, being particularly pleased about her manager's compliments on her organisation of a conference. Again she was posted a copy of the session notes, carefully phrased in tentative language and identifying more potential. She cancelled the third session on the grounds that she was too busy wrapping up work before leaving for her trip abroad. Two days later her employer called in to say that she was 'a new person'. O'Connell (1998) comments that solution-focused approaches have a great deal to offer employee-based assistance programmes in that they are economical in every sense of the word.

Shifting the locus of control

Many counsellors feel threatened by children who are referred by school, especially if the problems are behavioural and parents are less than helpful. In our experience solution-focused and narrative approaches provide a way of working that frequently makes the task enjoyable; children can really get into the method and make it exciting, and sometimes remarkable. We believe this is facilitated by the manner in which, as Ziegler (SFT e-mail list, 1998) says, the approach helps them to talk about meaningful change and what will be different when they have solved the problem that brought them to counselling – or when their parents or teachers would say they don't need to come anymore. He tells of a boy who had 'school phobias' (which two 'expert' child therapists had been unable to affect), who figured out in two sessions how to make school more fun by developing a strategy he used in sport. He had been afraid to go onto the playing field in case he made a mistake but then reminded himself that it was fun to be on the team and he could make it more fun by playing in certain ways.

Applying this solution to the phobia, he drew graphs of the 'fun ratio' and the 'fear ratio', showing how the former went up as the latter came down. The issue was lack of fun, not excess fear. This is another good example of needing to have a goal that is about starting something rather than ending something. Buchanan's (1999) overview of what works for troubled children confirms the effectiveness of interventions that recognise the positive qualities of young people and acknowledges that parents are more likely to be dispirited than resistant.

Working on a 'Raising Achievement' project at a high-school, two counsellors were asked to give counselling support to the eight most difficult and underachieving students. This work was discussed individually with each of those selected and they were given a choice as to whether to attend; the solution-focused and narrative approach was briefly explained and their views and concerns listened to. The pupils decided that they wanted to bring a friend and they agreed to select one each from the group, forming pairs of counsellees. These pairs were seen weekly for six sessions of 20 minutes. It quickly became clear that they felt they had little control over their lives, except when they were causing trouble, so they struggled with questions such as, 'how did you do that?'

The counsellors drew on the work of Dupper (1998), Furman (Internet, 1999) and LaFontain *et al.* (Internet, 1999). A common theme in these works is the 'locus of control'; for many 'difficult' children control is seen as outside themselves and so what they do is seen by them as uncontrolled and therefore they 'can't help it'. They were helped to distinguish between feelings, words and acts; between accepting that feelings were okay and they were not accountable for them, but that words and acts might not be okay and they were always accountable for these. The counsellors stressed that the pupils were not being blamed but they were being held accountable for their future behaviour; their education was in their hands and was too important to them to be messed up by others. Discussion often centred around what they were wrongly blamed for, how some hated being in school and could not wait to leave, how some were serious about doing well in school. Some were able to shift the locus of control and say, 'it's up to me, really' or, 'I've learned that if a teacher starts, I don't need to start back'; 'I like coming to school now – I want to do well'. There were interesting comments on oppressions such as bullying: 'This school can't cope with bullies'; 'Nowt gets sorted – it gets worse, if owt'; 'Bullies get away with it'. A sense of powerlessness was evident but scaled questions helped them to get a grip of the seriousness of problems, their own motivation to change and their confidence in their ability to do this. One boy developed his own solution to the bullying problem: 'we should have films to show what its like and have people talk about what they have been through'.

For some of these children it was their last year at school and this was talked of as a unique window of opportunity to learn a skill: 'Which skill would be the most useful to them?' This idea of skills came from Furman (www.reteaming.com) who begins by agreeing a nickname for the problem, then he looks for its corresponding skill and gives that a name. Pupils are asked to concentrate on the one skill they wish they could develop and consider what benefits it will give to the child and the environment, what new behaviour they will be displaying, what resources within them will be used to develop this skill, when has the child shown small bits of the skill, and other signs of progress lately; asking them to come up with some ideas that they wish to practise on, keeping it all light and playful. For example, one student felt 'messing about' was his biggest enemy, and he selected 'paying attention' as the skill he needed to develop.

Generally we find it easier to work with small groups because of the interpersonal nature of much 'complained-about' behaviour at school. Being cheeky to teachers is often encouraged by other pupils and the group or co-counsellee can help to counter that. Some teachers are regularly complained about by pupils – but it is possible to develop coping strategies and to shift the locus of control, as long as the work is done slowly and carefully. Lindsay was referred by Miss M., deputy head of Darkdale School, and arrived saying she wondered why she had to come. The counsellor said she didn't have to come unless it was her wish. Lindsay then said she thought it was because Miss M. found her behaviour improved after her last counselling but it had slipped to such an extent that she was now threatened with permanent exclusion. She was unclear as to how she had slipped so far, other than she was being sent out of lessons by the dreaded Mr F. (a much complained-about teacher at this school, but Lindsay had been storied as a pupil with problems due the fact that she lived with her grandmother after having been rejected by her parents) and out of the school, none of which was her fault, she claimed. Despite Mr F.'s probable unfairness, she was clear that she wanted to stay at this school and improve her performance. When asked what she thought Miss M. expected from her so that she could stay at Darkdale, she replied 'be on my best behaviour'. She was unable to elaborate on what that might be like so she was asked some scaling questions.

She rated herself at 10 on attendance; 7 on getting on with her work, 6/7 on messing about in class, and 6 for giving lip. Messing about in class caused the most problems for her, particularly with Mr F. and a supply teacher. Exceptions were sought – what was she doing differently in other classes so as not to get sent out? She answered this back to front, saying that in the problematic classes she was with her friends who wind her up, but sometimes she starts messing about:

[In this example, the series of questions, if read quickly, will look like an interrogation. In our practice, however, these questions are asked very slowly and tentatively, with a respectful not-knowing attitude. You may wish to practice this as you read the conversations.]

Counsellor: Which class is the easiest to behave well in?
Lindsay: English and PE.
Counsellor: What are you doing differently in English that helps you to behave?
Lindsay: Don't know, I can just behave.
Counsellor: How do you do behaving?
Lindsay: I just walk into the class and I am quiet . . . sit down and get on with it.
Counsellor: What if anyone starts winding you up in English?
Lindsay: She doesn't tell me off straight away. She says 'stop it', but she's right nice to me.
Counsellor: In what ways is she right nice to you?
Lindsay: Like, gives me stuff to do instead of the lesson – picks me to put pictures up. When I say I can't read in front of the class, she doesn't make me do it. Lets me do it when everyone has gone.
Counsellor: When she says 'stop it' do you?
Lindsay: Yes.
Counsellor: How do you do this?
Lindsay: She'll say 'stop it' and if I carry on she'll say 'both of you stop it'.
Counsellor: Fairness is important to you?
Lindsay: Don't know, think so.
Counsellor: How is it different in Mr F.'s class?
Lindsay: We all get together and have a laugh. When he says 'pay attention' we start giving him lip. Mostly he picks on me.
Counsellor: How is it different when it is a supply teacher?
Lindsay: I don't know – I can't get away with stuff – I don't care.
Counsellor: So you don't get away with it?
Lindsay: Not really.
Counsellor: What do you need to do to stay at Darkdale?
Lindsay: Don't shout in the corridors, don't distract people in class-rooms, don't knock on doors and run away. Stop cheeking dinner ladies. Keep right with Mr F. And don't bully people.
Counsellor: This is all 'don't do', what can you do instead?
Lindsay: The opposite to them.

Counsellor: So, what's the opposite to shouting in the corridor?
Lindsay: Don't do it.
Counsellor: That's not an opposite – what instead?
Lindsay: Bite my nails.
Counsellor: Tell me more about the shouting.
Lindsay: I do it 'cos I like doing it. I like singing loud, singing very loud. Dr Dre and stuff like that. Teachers can hear through the window and I shout at people through the windows.
Counsellor: What can you do instead of that?
Lindsay: Keep in my classroom and don't go in other classrooms – be supervised by a teacher all the time.
Counsellor: Or you could walk down the corridor on your hands – you couldn't sing then.
Lindsay: I can't walk on my hands.
Counsellor: Do you know how to do walking down the corridor without singing?
Lindsay: Depends on who's there. Like with some people I'm real quiet.
Counsellor: Who are these people?
Lindsay: Depends who I see.
Counsellor: Is it about showing off?
Lindsay: No. I like singing but when some people are there I'm not shy, but in front of some others I don't like to sing.
Counsellor: Is singing reasonable in corridors?
Lindsay: Well they should have double glazing, shouldn't they?
Counsellor: I don't think so.
Lindsay: My voice goes through that 'n all.

Feeling stuck, the counsellor decided to declare 'not knowing' and to be puzzled for quite a while as a way of inviting Lindsay to be creative and less defensive. Lindsay talked then of the teachers who shout at her; one had shouted, 'I've a good mind to get you kicked out of this school'. More puzzlement:

Counsellor: Miss M. noticed you had improved before; what were you doing that made her notice that?
Lindsay: I don't know.
Counsellor: In what areas did your behaviour improve?
Lindsay: Don't know but **she** saw an improvement.
Counsellor: You didn't?

Lindsay: No.

Counsellor: So, tell me if this is the scenario at school – the teachers get on to Miss M. about you and then she talks to you and then you get cheeky with her too?

Lindsay: I say it's not just me but I get done and they don't. She says 'I'm talking to you here, not them' and I say 'it's not just me'.

Counsellor: So how do those others get away with it?

Lindsay: Don't know. When she shouts.

Counsellor: So you don't want to give in on singing and shouting?

Lindsay: No. 'Cos that's what I like doing.

Counsellor: Who wins?

Lindsay: They probably do.

Counsellor: Is it worth it?

Lindsay: No.

Counsellor: How would you like to be at school?

Lindsay: What do you mean?

Counsellor: What would you like Miss M. to be saying about you?

Lindsay: I wouldn't want her to be saying I'm proper bad, just I've got a problem with corridors and teachers. Not, 'she does this and she does that'.

Counsellor: What's the biggest problem?

Lindsay: Teachers.

Counsellor: Has this problem got a name?

Lindsay: Don't know.

Counsellor: What does the problem make you do?

Lindsay: Don't know.

Counsellor: Do you cheek people everywhere?

Lindsay: Sometimes.

Counsellor: And there are consequences?

Lindsay: Yes.

Counsellor: You want to be different but the same?

Lindsay: Yes. [thoughtfully] It's really complicated.

Counsellor: It's a tricky one, Lindsay. How can you keep the good bits and lose the bad bits?

Lindsay: Don't know.

And so, back to scaled questions – she rated herself both happy and sad on the happiness scale and the counsellor agreed that's complicated too. She was 7/8 on 'the best person she could be' scale. This gentle search for exceptions encouraged Lindsay to lean forward and think hard about her behaviour. Great care was taken in the construction of her follow-up notes:

PROBLEM

Miss M. noticed that Lindsay's behaviour improved for a while but she has been annoying teachers by singing loudly in the corridors; shouting at people in other classrooms; knocking on doors and running away; cheeking dinner ladies; and Mr F. and the supply teacher; arguing with Miss M. about getting done when she is not the only pupil to misbehave. Some of these things happen at her Grandma's too.

EXCEPTIONS/PROGRESS

1   Lindsay doesn't get sent out of English or PE. She just walks into English and gets on with her work. When she is told to stop it by the teacher she is able to do this.
2   Her school attendance is very good.
3   Lindsay came to counselling and was very honest about her behaviour.
4   She can do good behaviour but she doesn't know how she does this except that she knows that it is more likely when she is treated with respect.

THOUGHTS ON SOLUTIONS

Lindsay is a bit short on solutions because doing best behaviour is very complicated for her. She wants to stay the same (enjoying singing and being loud and cheeky) but she also wants to change (but not turn into a swot). Lindsay has had so many lectures about her behaviour that she has forgotten all the good things about herself. This is not helping because it makes her feel both sad and happy. The good thing is that she is a fighter – she rates herself at 7/8 on 'the best person she could be' scale. We should be able to use this good quality to find a solution.

HOMEWORK

Lindsay will take a notepad to school and ask her teachers to write down all the good things she should keep at the front of the book and the bad things she should lose at the back of the book. She will start with the teachers she gets on with and work up to Mr F. She might ask her Grandma to write something too.

This homework is to help Judith and Lindsay work out all the good things about her so that she can do more of these. Lindsay doesn't need any more lectures at the moment as she has stopped listening to these.

AFTERTHOUGHTS

It will be tricky working out how Lindsay can do enough naughtiness to keep her personality without getting her into trouble. Naughtiness can be fun so we will have to think hard about where are the best places to do it and have fun without trouble.

Covering letter:

Dear Lindsay

As promised, here is a copy of your notes. I hope I have got them right because your situation is very complicated. If I have got anything wrong, please tell me next time we meet so that I can make any necessary alterations.

I hope the notepad is going well. I can think of lots of good things about you; for starters, you have a lively personality, you are a good singer and footballer and you care about getting an education. I expect there will be lots more which other people can write down. As you like Dr Dre, I'm lending you one of my CDs but please don't sing this one at school. It is guaranteed to annoy teachers. You can let me have it back sometime.

The counsellor knew that little could be done about Mr F. until after a vital Ofsted inspection, but wrote to Miss M. asking her to note any improvements in Lindsay's behaviour. There was no reply to this letter but Lindsay reported at the next session that the whole class had cheered when Mr F. announced that he would be leaving. Lindsay had asked him to write in her notepad and he only managed a grudging, 'not been in much trouble this lesson', although Lindsay reported that she had made a special effort in his class. She is still in school and managing to retain her 'personality'. She decided that there are 10 steps to exclusion and that she will be safe if she does not go over 'step 8'. She worked out what to do to stay at 'step 8' by 'borrowing' a bit of a life she admired – a pupil who was well liked by both staff and pupils. The counsellor had no idea what these 'steps' actually were but this didn't matter as Lindsay had a workable solution.

Susie equally felt oppressed by people with power over her, with work pressures then impacting on her health more generally. Her flashbacks of earlier sexual abuse were exacerbated by sitting alone in her flat all day, but she hesitated to return to work as she was criticised by her manager for not following instructions properly. She had been using her commonsense in working out what to do when she could not follow his poor explanations but this hadn't always worked well for her. Although Susie's confidence in her work ability was low, she was not given a pretend task. Exception exploration revealed that she could follow instructions when they were given clearly and she was able to identify an older, woman manager who always gave such instructions. Here it was important not only to separate the person from the problem, but also locate the problem elsewhere; many work or school environments are unfair and have to be tolerated – but not always. Susie decided that she would ask the woman colleague to observe her taking instructions from the male manager and then give her advice. As expected, it was the male manager who received advice on the giving of instructions, not Susie. This small act of assertion on Susie's part was important in her subsequent recovery from the effects of prolonged sexual abuse.

Coping with stress through discovering new skills

As in the case of Lindsay's complex relationship with school, many people become stressed at work because of interpersonal difficulties with peers or those people who have informal power over them, such as longer-serving staff. The oppression experienced, and the distress caused by it, seems all the worse because of its intangible nature. For example, Jim had adapted to work well and was proud of his ability to undertake complex jobs and work long hours, but he could not get on with an older man who conveyed criticism without ever putting this into words. Jim could only describe this as being made to feel 'discomfortable', although the feeling was so intense he had walked out of work without explanation when in the middle of a job with this man. He was at risk of losing his job because of this and, as some work involved him in travelling in a lorry with this man, Jim was feeling trapped and worried that he would 'explode'.

Exception-finding produced one workable solution – he had coped with some journeys by talking resolutely about the job rather than the more usual workmate banter, but this made the situation no more than tolerable. Jim was asked to toss a coin of his choice each evening. He identified the 'horse' side as the one he liked best so that was selected as a signal to pretend all day that he was such a competent worker that he could not possibly be criticised by the older man; indeed, the man would be amazed by how good his work was. He was also asked to list his work skills on the pretend days on a 'well-done' card to be kept on his fridge door. This simple homework was sufficient for Jim to identify his skills and achievements, thus preventing any sense of being 'put down' by the older worker. Externalising 'discomfortableness' also led to Jim exploring a sense of unease and lack of confidence in other areas of his life, with a similar increase in self-confidence.

Unlike schoolchildren, adult workers can have unreasonable expectations of their ability to handle oppressive situations. Denise was an experienced youth worker who came for counselling to deal with her feelings of powerlessness after a gang of youths threatened her late one evening after she refused to give them a lift. Although this had been a potentially dangerous and frightening experience (two youths sat in her car uninvited whilst the others rocked it), she said her problem was

> to feel more confident in myself. As for the situation I went through, I dealt with it well professionally but not personally. I felt very powerless. I'm concerned that it might happen again. I don't feel confident enough that I could deal with it.

In some respects the oppression she suffered consisted of direct personal threats but the professional expectation that she could handle difficult youths exacerbated her sense of oppression, causing her to locate the problem within herself rather than in the support arrangements made by her employers. When asked what would be a good outcome for her, she was able to say putting her personal safety first and forgetting everything else (the professional expectations). This enabled her to devise a sensible safety plan which did not involve her in developing skills in diffusing potentially dangerous situations. Reasonable and realistic responsibility-taking would, she decided, involve the following action on her part:

1 She will park her car near other workers and near brightly lit, busy areas such as shops.

2 She will check that all workers leave together and drive off at the same time.

3 She will consider closing the club and re-siting the project in a safer area.

4 She will not open up clubs on her own (this is the caretaker's job anyway). She will arrive and leave with her co-workers.

5 She will raise safety issues with her managers, particularly the siting of clubs in badly lit, dangerous areas. If they take no action, she will refuse to work in these areas.

6 She will save her skills in diffusing situations for in-club work or where she meets one or two young people outside. If she encounters more than two young people outside in the dark (however friendly they seem), she will walk away from the situation.

She returned for the second session delighted at her managers' response to her requests (they had not only agreed her plan but taken the onus away from her having to explain the new safety arrangements to the other workers, and provided her with a mobile phone), but distressed by a further episode of threatened violence. On her return to work, the same youths had banged on the club doors, broken the locks on the doors, and then climbed onto the roof. The police had been called but only questioned the youths and then asked them to move on. This had brought back all her feelings of upset and anger. She was clearer about feeling unprotected but also sad about the possibility of the community losing its much-needed youth facility.

Interestingly, her preferred outcome this time was wider than previously, although still within what could be reasonably and realistically achieved. Her aim was to take action that would make life safer for everyone on the estate (and *de facto* for services in the area) by arranging a community meeting to which she would also invite the local police and housing officers. To meet her personal needs, she chose a self-pampering programme as she had been neglecting her home life for her professional duties. Acknowledging the complexities of power in her situation and emphasising the limits of personal responsibility-taking enabled Denise to take more responsibility for both her own, and others', safety; allowing her to develop both professionally and personally as a youth worker in a deprived community.

To conclude, the most important aspect of work with schoolchildren and workers is, we suggest, to recognise that they are attempting to *solve* a problem rather than stop *being* a problem. That problem is rarely a single issue. Using a narrative approach in combination with a solution-focused approach enables both client and counsellor to identify the multifaceted sources of oppression that are sustaining the problem's life.

8

Personal safety and well-being

Before reading this chapter we invite you to rate yourself on the following scales:

- If 0 is not at all and 10 is completely satisfied, how do you feel about how you look?
- If 0 is not at all and 10 is all the time, how much time do you spend thinking about, or discussing with friends and colleagues, how best you can manage your health?
- If 0 is never and 10 is every other month, how often have you started either a new diet or exercise regime?

We suspect that your scores are likely to be below halfway on the first scale, and above halfway on the others, particularly if you are a woman. We are so bombarded with stories about healthy lifestyles and desirable body shapes that many people tell us that they will be happier when they are thinner or have changed the way they look. Their acceptance of a happiness through thinness story is such that they not only struggle to say what they would be *doing* differently when they achieve this goal, but they are surprised that we even ask the question. As Smith *et al.* say: 'Even when we outwardly reject the cultural norms, many of us are still left with internalised feelings of inadequacy, of not quite "measuring up"' (Smith *et al.*, 1998: 6).

So how does a counsellor decide whether a person's goal of changing their body is an ethical goal? How does she decide what constitutes self-harm when altering one's body can be socially constructed as simultaneously desirable and undesirable, healthy and unhealthy? For example, slimming and exercise to reduce obesity is promoted as healthy, but 'excessive' dieting and exercise is frowned upon; body piercing and tattooing has different social connotations depending largely on the social class or fame of an individual person; and, when does an enema become colonic irrigation? And not only are our body shapes the subject of endless media, government and medical narratives, but increasingly more of our emotional states and behaviours are being storied as 'dysfunctions' that require medical interventions. For children these include ADHD and dyslexia; for men they include a variety of compulsive disorders; and for women they include eating disorders and self-harm. No wonder that we view ourselves with dissatisfaction; we are most of us misshapen in some way by 'thin' health stories.

The diagnoses and labels which accompany these stories can seem helpful as we seek to understand ourselves better; not least in that they provide an excuse for our behaviours and a respite from responsibility-taking. However, they also take control away from us, placing it in the hands of experts. If the prescribed 'expert' treatment fails to work, the person is left with nothing more than a stigmatising label (for a fuller discussion, see Furman and Ahola, 1992; Weakland, 1993). Not surprisingly, people come to resent or resist such identities, particularly if there is an element of permanence or incurability about them. Clients do not find negative or rigid definitions of themselves useful or motivating. Added to this they also carry the burden of failed professional hopes. For example, Shona was more distressed by comments from nurses about her cutting than she was about the distress and pain that led her to cut herself in the first place:

> When I go to A&E, they say straight off, 'which arm is it this time, Shona?' I feel *that* big. It's so embarrassing. I try not to go to hospital now but the stitching helps. It distracts me from the thoughts. Not being able to go leaves me coping with a bad patch on my own.

The nurses' attitude was understandable but, as Smith *et al.* (1998) comment, it invalidates the means by which Shona had found to communicate something extremely painful about which she could not speak openly, and a way of coping which was helpful to her. It also ran the danger of deterring her from seeking treatment for what were very deep cuts.

At the same time as more behaviours are being classified as syndromes and disorders, so is an idealised-family healthy lifestyle increasingly promoted. The burden of these narratives falls most heavily on women, whose ways of being a desirable young woman or a good mother are most closely prescribed. Why is pre-conceptual care expected of women but not men? Ingleby (1984) refers to the way women internalise professional narratives about pregnancy and childcare as a total institution without walls. Allied to current notions of providing care in the community, this gives women more responsibility but less support. 'Community care' suggests interconnectedness and mutual support but community facilities are largely determined and organised by men and 'community becomes women's *place*, the place to which they are relegated and belong' (Williams, 1993: 34), rather than *space* in which to make choices and exercise responsibility. Little wonder then that many of the women we see are filled with self-blame for failing to live up to the prescriptions of experts who monitor their families' health and well-being.

White (1995) considers all theories of health as problematic because they specify lives and relationships, but he does think it helpful to clarify people's ideas and practices of health on the grounds that:

> This knowledge also makes it possible for us [counsellors] to join with people in an exploration of those aspects of their life that they might be able to appreciate but that don't fit with these notions of health and normality. As some of these aspects become more visible to people, they are more able to honour their refusal to subject their lives to the ideas and practices that are informed by dominant notions of health and normality. (White, 1995: 139–40)

This is very much our rationale in this chapter. While we recommend externalising internalised health stories in our counselling work, we have no notion of health other than what works best for each person within the limits of reasonable responsibility-taking.

Reclaiming self-hood

The possible damaging effects of sexual abuse on self-hood are well-documented (see, for example, Durrant and Kowalski, 1990; Dolan, 1991, 1998a, Madge, 1997). In some forms of counselling the emphasis is on talking through the feelings or even reliving the experience with a view to coming to terms with it. We are quite concerned about the effects of such work and we have met people who seem to have been further abused, as it were, by this process. White advises against reliving traumas as this 'can reinforce dominant meanings' (1995: 86) and lead to more self-hate. In order to avoid further harm we begin with a basic question, 'What would you like to get out of counselling?' or with the miracle question or some version of a future-goal question, talking about a *reclaimed* life as soon as possible. Abused people often have a great deal of anger towards the perpetrator and a wish to get revenge. We would discuss how this revenge might help recovery and what will be different, as talking at length about taking action, such as going to court, means that the abuser remains in control of the client's life and thoughts. We like Dolan's comment that living well is the best revenge because it counters the domination of the abuser on the person's life. By asking questions like, 'what do you think needs to happen here for this to be useful to you?' we can check how much discussion of history will be helpful and whether it will constitute a second abusive experience. We may add that remembering pleasant things or successes in one's life can be a good start because it can counterbalance the troubling things: 'so what is happening that you want to continue happening?' Then we write these things down to show their importance for the recovery story. A solution focus is introduced by a question like, 'What will be the first sign that things are getting better for you even a little bit, or has it already happened?' (Dolan, 1998b).

We also seek to avoid generalisations and assumptions that an abusive experience is the same for any two people, listening carefully to their wants and feelings. In one person it may be a need to stop flashbacks, in another a need to get family support or to move to a safer place. And not everyone is severely damaged by abuse. The effects are less where disclosures are positively received, where family and friends are supportive (Madge, 1997), and where mothers are supported (Peake and Fletcher, 1997). Some people are more devastated by disbelief and unhelpful responses to disclosure than the actual abuse. For example, David said:

> I coped with it in my own way for years. Maybe I covered it up but since it came out . . . my cousin rang Child Line . . . it's been terrible. 'Cos of the court case, I had to tell my bosses and my mate keeps telling me he doesn't think I'm gay! And my uncle . . . I looked up to him but he's siding with 'him'. I couldn't believe what he was saying. I just went out and got drunk.

People who have been sexually abused often feel that their bodies are no longer their own or regard them as contaminated (for a fuller discussion see Milner, 2001), and this can lead to self-harming, reckless sexual behaviour and suicide attempts. Abused people often need to be helped to value and appreciate themselves again by first identifying times when they experience good physical feelings such as the pleasure of soaking in a bath or the bodily awareness that dancing can bring, provided it is free of sexual connotations. Shona, for example, had difficulty in looking at her body and showered with the light off ('I think of my body as really dirty'), so she opted for a bath-time routine which consisted of a cool shower with perfumed soap (medicated soap had connotations with the original abuse) to wash off the 'dirt' and imagine it going down the plug-hole. She would then have a warmer shower with her favourite unperfumed soap and dry herself with a fluffy towel. What we call 'bedroom therapy' can also help people who find sleep difficult when the bedroom is associated with the abuse. Clients are encouraged to plan how to make their bedroom feel more warm and safe; for example, David simply needed to sleep on the other side of his bed, away from the door; while other people change the entire decoration or even move the furniture about and add some comfort symbols that remind them of enjoyable times. Although we developed these ideas in response to abused people's feelings of disgust with their bodies and intrusive thoughts, we have also found them useful in our work with violent men. Their internalised narratives are different; they are burdened with stories of being fit, tough guys and they often find that they can be tender and considerate to others after they have become more tender and considerate to their own bodies. Individually designed self-pampering programmes marvellously subvert many of the problem narratives around 'health'.

Personal agency is very difficult to keep alive during traumatic abuse – some people feel it died. Yet there is always some inner resistance of which the person can be proud, the storying of which helps to counter the story of spoilt identity: 'Internalising a view of self as helpless and powerless is not an inevitable outcome' (Adams-Westcott, Daffron and Sterne (1993: 262). The meaning that is ascribed to the event is crucial; such as, who is responsible, who is disqualified by it, what does it say about those involved?: 'If a person is recruited into a negative story about who they are as a person, then it is likely that they will give meanings to their experiences that emphasise culpability and worthlessness' (White 1995: 84). Therefore the story often focuses on low self-worth, self-blame and lack of control, editing out alternative knowledge of self in a restricted inner conversation. Accessing and developing an alternative conversation which includes recalling lost qualities, and being affirmed by a respectful conversation, helps to restore self-respect:

> Our primary task is to assist these people to derive alternative meanings of their experiences of abuse, to step into some other more positive account of who they might be as a person. There are expressions of experience that bring with them very different effects on the shape of lives, effects that are constructive rather than destructive . . . this reinterpretation will change the shape of the expression of people's experiences of abuse and therefore the shape of their lives. This reinterpretation is not forced by the therapist but is generated collaboratively. (White, 1995: 84)

For example, 'You knew what he was doing was wrong', 'You were too small to stop him but you were really clear about what was right and what was wrong' (Durrant, 1997) can help in resurrecting personal agency and self-respect. Similarly, Holme (2000) suggests to young people who attend a group for young women abused from an early age that their nightmares were a sign of resistance; this being the only way in which very young children can protest. Many people are able to change the ending of a nightmare once the possibility is raised, although it is important that the person chooses their own ending. We have also found that many young abused people talk about water as an escape from the abuse; for example, David said: 'When the thoughts come, I go to the baths and swim as hard as I can. Then I do a length under the water. I feel safe doing that.' Again this is storied as resistance. White says that abused people sometimes lose discernment and confuse contradictory experiences such as love/exploitation, care/ neglect, nurture/abuse, because 'to experience abuse in contexts that are designated as loving and caring is both mystifying and confusing' (1995: 93). Talking about unique outcomes helps discernment develop, these outcomes being the seeds of the counterplot. He asks, 'Does this fit with abuse or care?, self-abuse or self-care?', finding that as people become more in touch with self and life they become able to take safety measures' (1995: 94).

As part of showing respect, we suggest that clients be invited to decide for themselves whether talking about the abuse would be helpful or oppressive. Dolan (1991) maintains that pathologising patterns that may have served some purpose in the past need to be externalised and the abuse seen in a context of oppression. People can be helped to map how their lives have been limited by disqualifying beliefs and to draft a new map for the future, a future in which the problem does not flow from a deficit in them but from oppressive forces elsewhere, against which they have been heroic. At least some uncertainty about the negative story occurs and possibilities for a new identity story begin to grow. Dolan (1998b) has also developed many therapeutic tasks, such as comfort cues, 'consulting the wise sage within', letters from the future, and letters to write, read and burn. Part of Shona's letter (not for posting) to her abusive brother said:

> It's about time you faced up to what you did. But somehow the victim suffers. They are the ones who feel bad for something which was out of their control. But you've always been good at that, the way you used to call me your naughty little sister. You sang that Heavy Metal song, 'I know a thing or two about my little sister', and that made me feel like I was guilty. I can't stand you and I can't stand what you did to me and believe me, your day will come. I hope one day you're in the same situation I was in where you feel frightened, powerless and where you don't know what is going to fucking happen next like I did when you abused me. This is the last fucking time you'll hear from me as you're nothing but a paedophile. Good luck in your sad life 'cos you're gonna need it.

At the next session she reported that she realised how the song line had supported her sense of self-blame for many years but she felt free of it now. Durrant (1997) suggests placing the past in the future by asking, 'How will you know when you have worked through it enough?', 'When we have talked about what has happened as much as you need to, what will be different?', 'How will you decide what to talk about today?'

Fiona, for example, said that she would know she was better when she wasn't thinking and talking about the abuse so much, although she didn't know what sort of person she would be. She thought this a little scary at first but then commented that she would leave her options open to be any sort of person she wanted to be, and was delighted to discover that she had choices.

Violence

Men who commit violence often seek counselling when their partners threaten to leave them or they are due in court and, here, White (1993, 1995) has produced clear guidance (see also, Jenkins, 1990; Murphy, 1996). This includes inviting such men to take responsibility for the harm done, remembering when they felt vulnerable, identifying the effects of violence, developing an appropriate apology, committing to making amends, confronting patriarchal thinking and developing proposals for new relationships with women and children in which the men are accountable for setting up structures to make it easier, and more likely, for women to give feedback. Establishing a context for new ways of being men is of key importance. Externalisation of the attitudes and beliefs that support violence is part of the process, not externalisation of the violence itself as that would shift responsibility from men. Men may be asked, 'If a man desired to dominate another person, particularly a woman or child, what sort of attitudes would be necessary to achieve this?'; followed by, 'To what extent does he wish to cooperate with these ideas?.' 'When he does not cooperate with them, how does he feel?'

Lipchik (1988) has developed solution-focused practice with couples who want a violence-free relationship. As part of her work she develops a video-picture of the future without violence, on the basis that the most constructive influence is 'the influence of anticipation', making people open to their own resources. She uses questions like, 'What options do you have when you are angry?' Violence may be used when the partner becomes angry and it may be necessary to ask, 'How would you like her to deal with that in the future?', and the woman may be asked, 'How would you like him to deal with you when you are angry in the future?' Exceptions are sought: 'Tell me of a case where you found a way to compromise about your differences', 'How can you have a future relationship based on what you have learned about how relationships can be?'

In working with couples the agency needs to have clear guidelines for the counsellor's and the abused party's safety. The couple is required to have a strong commitment to a non-violent relationship. We prefer the abused partner to choose at what point to join the sessions, if at all; finding this most usually occurs after a small number of individual sessions have led to demonstrably different ways of the abuser behaving in the relationship. We have found this to be particularly important when dealing with same-sex violence as lesbians, in particular, have a strong commitment to keeping the relationship even where the violence is severe (Renzetti, 1992; Leventhal and Lundy, 1999).

Morrow and Hawxhurst (1998) emphasise not only that it is the survivor, not the batterer or counsellor, who initiates readiness for couples counselling, but also that the counsellor makes clear their familiarity with the dynamics of couples violence.

The assessment of safety and of motivation is difficult and often complicated by the use of drink or drugs. It is important to evaluate progress from sources other than just the perpetrator and to see that signs of safety are being increased. We use the scale in Appendix 3d, asking the perpetrator, and any others who are available, to complete it at intervals.

Suicidal and self-harming clients

These clients seem to attract scorn in many hospitals. Presumably because their harm is self-inflicted, they are often disrespected by busy medics. They also cause some anxiety because threats of suicide are sometimes carried out; Seton-Browne (SFT e-mail list, 2000) claims that 10 per cent do complete suicide. Such threats make it harder to listen to goals. For some desperate people, however, suicide is sometimes seen as the only choice they have left in life; the only way to maintain a sense of control; or a way of ending pain. One young woman explained that cutting put her in control of the amount of pain she suffered, whilst another said that she got relief from seeing the blood flow. They both viewed their cutting as a way of coping. While we do not seek a theory of suicide or cutting other than White's (1995: 83) comments above, we strive to listen, despite the feelings the behaviour arouses in us, and ascertain what the client wants to achieve. It helps us to think that the behaviour is a way of telling us that they desperately want to change something. Rather than exploring the trouble we focus on future goals, trying to separate the behaviour from the goal which may have little to do with harming or dying. Discovering 'true intent' is difficult; it is always possible for people to kill or maim themselves by accident. Likewise failure to kill oneself does not necessarily mean lack of intent.

Therefore we take seriously what the client says and ask if there are other ways to achieve their goals. We seek to clarify the aim behind the action and ask, 'how will that make things better?' and, 'can we think of some alternatives?' Odd as it may seem, death may be an interim goal; we can, however, become interested in their overall or long-term goals. We can ask suppositional questions such as, 'suppose your overall goal (for example, getting people off your back) is achieved, how will you know it has happened?', 'what will be different?' Here scaling questions can be creative in generating a sense of movement or gradual change; asking, 'What would the first step be, apart from self-harm?' (Hawkes, Marsh and Wilgosh 1998: 103). In accepting suicide as an alternative means, the client is supported in an overall goal, but self-harm can be questioned as an option by, for example, asking 'This option seems very hard on yourself – do you deserve that?' Macdonald (SFT e-mail list, 2000) asks, 'What was the (for example, the overdose) about?' If the reply is, 'I was fed up', he asks, 'Did the overdose help?' If the reply is, 'Yes', he asks, 'what could you do *instead* next time that would be easier on you?' Berg (SFT e-mail list, 1999) says, 'You must have a good reason for hurting yourself', and she then goes on to explore what a better solution might look like. Callcott (SFT e-mail list, 2000) asks about past coping and seeks to build on such 'exceptions'. She also asks, 'suppose in six months or so, you were to look back and see this meeting as something that turned out to be for the best, how will you know?, and 'what will you be doing differently?' Hope can be built while avoiding blame. When people say that death would be preferable to their present situation, we ask them for evidence of this.

The approach we have described above may seem to be risky; all self-harm has potentially fatal consequences. Measuring and quantifying risk is difficult, however, and while referring a client to another service may seem the safest professional option, it merely shifts the responsibility away from the counsellor and client. We prefer to focus on *safety*, which is much more measurable as it does not consist of a void (for a fuller discussion, see Turnell and Edwards, 1999). Scaled questions are the simplest way of assessing safety; for example with suicidal clients, 'If 0 is not at all and 100 is completely, how interested in the future are you?' At the heart of safety work, however, are notions of personal responsibility-taking. We have mentioned several times that women, in particular, take on responsibilities which are unreasonable and unrealistic so we do not let the client set the lead in goal-setting where there are serious safety concerns.

Holding people accountable for *safety* rather than for harm seems to be effective, be it for their own safety or for that of others affected by their violence. We also look at harm while balancing it against occasions when it did not happen, 'What else can you do?', 'What else can others do?', 'What else can I do?' Rather than seeking to understand pathology or symptoms, we focus on and encourage 'non-problem' talk.

Eating management – creating balance

Healthy eating and dieting narratives are potentially fatal. For people with eating disorders, Jacob (2001) says that food is a wolf in sheep's clothing – we need food to live but food is also the enemy from which there is no escape. This makes people feel hopeless. Externalising internalised narratives for people with severe weight loss is particularly difficult as chaotic eating patterns make for chaotic thinking processes. Jacob externalises undereating as a jealous liar that says, 'stay with me, I'll keep you safe', but this is no more than a comfort blanket is for a child; one that gets dirtier and smellier from being dragged along the floor but resists being thrown away. Sonya, for example, described it as a monster:

> I can't really see it. I think the monster's anorexia and it's male . . . because it's not a she or an it. It fills my stomach and controls my mind. I don't know whether it's an enemy or a friend. It's very clever. [Long pause as she struggled to put her thoughts into words.] There's three bits to it . . . Sonya-the-person, the monster, and sort of hybrid Sonya–monster. They all get confused in my mind. When I eat normally, it says 'Oh, you've eaten that. Don't have your next meal'. It's too strong for me to stand up to. It doesn't mind me coming for counselling because it knows it won't work.

Some of these clients are referred by others who are concerned about them and it is crucial to check out what the referred person wants from counselling. De Shazer (1994) asks such a client how the referrer will know when to stop worrying. The reply may be, 'When I am able to eat a meal'. He would then ask 'Once?', and go on to check out the required period of time; and does it mean eating and keeping it down. Of course referrers usually cannot say how long the eating would need to continue before they knew the problem was solved. They often want something else like 'tolerance of food' or 'feeling better about eating' or 'having more energy'. He would continue to tease out what would be different that would indicate these goals had been reached before looking for exceptions or discussing when last the client was like that. He would then ask the miracle question to lead into the future solution without having to bother about the 'how' of getting there. By discussing life when the client is eating normally the details become 'fact-like' (de Shazer, 1994: 225), the solution state is experienced, and possibilities are created and amplified with questions like, 'What else would be different?', 'How would it affect others?' and, 'What would they be saying and doing that would be different?' For example, Sonya's goal was not to be worried about food anymore, not to have it hanging over her 24 hours a day, so she was asked what she would be doing with her thoughts when she wasn't using them up worrying about eating. This conversation can be quite light and imaginative and clients can surprise themselves with their own ideas. Progress scales can then be used to thicken the new story. The session may end with verbal feedback after a break or, in our case, with a written feedback as soon as possible.

The narrative approach externalises undereating to enable a protest to start against its pervasive influence and reduce self-pathologising. As various taken-for-granted cultural factors are identified, considering the 'recruitment' process further externalises the problem. Thus the modes of life and thought that shape lives, the 'history of the present', is discussed. This provides space for the client to see through the 'ruses' that have tricked the client into certain attitudes towards the body. The client is then invited to make a choice between submitting to the problem or challenging it. White calls this 'bifurcation'; asking a question such as, 'Are you content to submit to the problem or are you attracted to the idea of challenging it?' (Tomm 1993: 69). This question realigns the client's emotional commitment and empowers the client to protest against the problem. Jacob (2000) aids this process by suggesting that the problem's invitations can be resisted by giving it a 'direct line'; saying something like, 'I hear you but get on your way'. As clients gradually articulate a vision of a preferred future they are more able to take steps towards it. The new story is further strengthened by extending the 'audience'; discussing the involvement of others or telling others about the new vision.

Dolan (1997) has approached overeating in a similar way. Most of these clients are self-referred and well-motivated, and therefore the start is usually straightforward. We know that diets usually fail; 95 per cent of dieters regain the weight they lose (Gullo, 1995) and many gain additional weight. However no-one overeats always. By use of a miracle question, lengthy discussion of the future without the problem, identification of exceptions, and scaling, the work proceeds as with most other problems. Daily or weekly sub-goals can be set. Dieting affects many aspects of a person's life and building the solution can involve activities of living that are not just about mealtimes. Dolan (1997), for example, has devised a Daily Solution-focused Weight Maintenance Success Scale that restories the situation in constructive language and broadens the focus through such statements as, 'I have spent some time relaxing unrelated to food', and, 'I spent some time today exploring creative interests unrelated to snacking or food'. One young woman told us that she found it easier to resist bingeing after she had worked out that negative thoughts weigh heavier than positive ones.

Like so many other difficulties for which people seek counselling, eating difficulties are often influenced by relationships. Selekman (1997) gives an example of a mother who worried about her son's overeating because his father was obese and had died of a heart attack. The boy felt that his mother's nagging seemed to lead to his 'pigging out' all the more, leaving him quite 'defeated' and distressed. Selekman spent some time with the boy visualising the future without overeating and setting solution-focused tasks – he secretly asked the boy to pretend to comply with his mother's wishes on eating over the next week and he, also secretly, asked the mother to 'do something different', with a view to disrupting the pattern of arguments. At the next session the boy had created several 'exceptions' which were built upon. This could be said to exemplify McFarland's (1995) philosophy of not pushing the process but letting the clients make the changes – just bringing them out in conversations.

Reauthoring psychiatric stories

Nowhere are problems more pathologised than in discussions of mental illness. Yet within the psychiatric profession there are those who are actively concerned about the potential danger of psychiatric labels. Hawkes, Marsh and Wilgosh (1998) say that after 15 years of professional practice they realise they do not know what words like psychosis, manic depression and schizophrenia mean. White (1995) maintains that psychotic experience, particularly, rules people out of contention in the stakes of personhood as they are constructed as objects of psychiatric knowledge. Furman and Ahola (1992) also suggest that psychiatric diagnoses become self-verifying and that 'watchful wording' can be helpful in preventing a person becoming a label. For example, they suggest that 'borderline personality disorder' is more helpfully described as 'a search for a new life direction'. Psychiatric theories of aetiology are not necessary for practice; what is necessary is to listen carefully to clients' knowledges and to talk in ways that promote personal agency.

There can be a therapeutic conversation that is not based on pathology. For example, de Shazer would use presuppositional language to develop a picture and an expectation of change, of life being a little better in whatever way is defined by the client as better. He would discuss ordinary human *complaints* rather than pathologies. This is not to deny that there are some people with extreme forms of deviant behaviour but it nevertheless questions the so-called norm from which they deviate and it permits the possibility of addressing people's everyday problems in a pragmatic way, looking at what happens and what the person wants, building on what they are able to do that is useful to them. This pragmatism about doing what works is wide enough to include psychiatric interventions such as ECT. This is reported to help some people and if it helps, it helps. The role of language in mental illness, however, needs to be addressed further and a diagnosis never tells enough – we need to engage the client in a detailed discussion of their relationship with the problem. Traditionally counsellors were wary of this form of engaging, fearing that the psychodynamic process would make matters worse and work was sometimes restricted to 'reality enforcement', but we would argue against this viewpoint. Rather than imposing a particular view of 'reality', counsellors can focus on what the client wants to be better in their lives, accepting their point of view so long as this acceptance does not become unlawful, dangerous or immoral. Hawkes, Marsh and Wilgosh (1998) say that if people have bizarre views they can be asked, 'how do you know this?', 'how do you think someone else would deal with this?,' 'could there be another explanation?', 'what do your family think about this?' We can also bypass explanations and ask how the client or their family would like things to be different in the future.

Delusional ideas are often linked to considerable fear and isolation, and so we can engage on this common ground, maintaining a common focus on health, safety and what needs to happen for the work to end.

Goals are often, therefore, about achieving peace, calm, more choices in life, trust, and less reliance on medication. Even if ideas about the problem and the ways of dealing with it are 'crazy', the goals are often 'sane'. De Shazer (SFT e-mail list, 2000) says that clients need the ability to hold a conversation to benefit substantially from counselling – a conversation being an exchange of information in a turn-taking manner. However, we find that even if a person does not seem to be 'making sense', if we assume that they *are* making sense then they seem to make sense more quickly, though some people need more time than others (Simon, SFT e-mail list, 1999).

This is particularly important when counselling people who report that they hear voices. All too often the counsellor panics at this point and refers the client to a psychiatrist without exploring what the voices mean to the client and what they are saying. No wonder, then, that the client becomes as fearful of the voices as the counsellor, or stops telling people about them. Getting detail about the voices a client hears enables them to understand the meaning of the voices to them and increases their resistance to voices which discredit and denigrate. White (1995) suggests that it is more helpful to question the purposes and motives of the voices; whether these are auditory hallucinations or the more generalised voices of psychiatric expertise, for example: 'Are these voices *for* you having an opinion or are they *against* you?'; 'These voices throw you into confusion. Whose interests are best served by this confusion?'; 'What is it like for the voices to have to listen to your thoughts for a change?'; and 'What is it like for them to know that you are developing a disrespect and mistrust of them?' We find that clients respond well to such conversations as this extract from a session with Ruth, a young woman who had made sufficient recovery from bingeing and self-harming after sexual abuse to return to university, shows:

> Ruth: I'm doing all right on my course but I'm taking these drugs. It says on the bottle that they're for acute and chronic schizophrenia. They get rid of the voices but they make me feel hung over 14 hours a day. The doctor says just take them at night but this doesn't help. They don't make me sleep any better and I feel dreadful all the time. When I complain, he says, 'so what's worse? Feeling groggy or having the voices? Don't complain.' Once they've written the prescription, that's it. End of interest. I'm still getting the voices on and off.

Counsellor: What are they saying to you?

Ruth: The same old stuff. Nothing new.

Counsellor: Dad's old criticisms?

Ruth: It's like a bloke's voice . . . not someone I recognise. Not dad's. It's very critical. Reinforces your insecurities.

Counsellor: What do you say back?

Ruth: My voice is sarcastic.

Counsellor: What do you think the purpose of this voice is, what does it want?

Ruth: When you start to achieve something, it's a constant reminder not to let you do it. I get ready to go out. Think, I'm up for this. And then the voices kick in and you don't go. And then feel worse for not going. When you decide not to go, you don't have to face it but . . . it's won. Stopped you doing it. Feel crap because people ask you out, you don't go and then they stop asking you. Think you're a mood-swinging person. It's difficult to explain ten minutes before going out. One housemate knows. She does the excuses for me.

Counsellor: Could she do anything else to help?

Ruth: She says, 'tell them to fuck off'. She doesn't agree with me taking the prescription. I take it for a few days and then cope for a few days.

Counsellor: How do you do coping on these days?

Ruth: Denial. It's like someone's talking in the background and it's there but I'm not listening . . . and that's really hard to do when there's important things to do. Can't say, I'm not going to write this essay.

Counsellor: What effect does it have on the voices when you stand up to them?

Ruth: It doesn't affect them. It has an effect on I how I feel . . . more positive. When I feel more positive I can go out. It doesn't make them go away.

As the voice was at its most disqualifying when Ruth was getting ready to go out (telling her she was disgustingly fat as she showered), she decided to give it a good hearing earlier in the day and a 'direct line' when she was in the shower, saying 'I've heard all that stuff this morning'. In this way, she was able to 'win' more frequently. Similarly, Shona began to argue with the voice that told her to cut herself. She was able to use the idea that the voice was repetitive and had nothing new to say to her by taunting it with this fact: 'I said, "I know I've done it hundreds of times before. Can't you think of anything else to say?" I've decided that there's only so many more cuts it's allowed.' By showing an interest in people's voices we have discovered that thoughts are often experienced as auditory hallucinations; indeed, it seems that this is a way by which people resist intrusive thoughts so blocking them with medication can actually be counterproductive.

Clients who are described as mentally ill will often be on courses of medication. A counsellor who is not medically qualified should not interfere with these treatments but can have useful conversations about what the person can do to make the medication work better for them. We can ask, 'What percentage of the progress is due to the pills and what percentage is due to you?', or 'What does the medication help you to *do*?', 'In what way does it enable *you* to have a better quality of life?', 'What else is its effect?' This reduces any sense of dependence on the drug and increases a sense of personal agency.

Many clients tell us that their problem is 'depression' as though it refers to something that has a real existence, but we feel it is important to consider that 'depression' is largely a linguistic construction 'held in place by consensual agreement in a "language game"' (Price, 1993: 277). So-called linguistic realities are constructed by the language that describes them. The words, 'You are a depressive', make a person into a thing whereas the words, 'You are under the influence of depression', make collaboration possible. Even when the depression is seen *as* a thing, one's relationship with it, and how the person can *be*, can be changed/re-storied. Furman and Ahola (1992), for example, prefer to describe depression as latent joy. We ask, 'how do you do depression?', 'what are you doing when you are not depressed?', 'when you have joy, what will you be doing?' as this represents a process or an interaction with self and others and it becomes possible to address what one could be doing instead. Of course there will be those who are so oppressed by experiences of abuse, so lacking in self-belief, and so lacking in social supports, that their generativity is seriously restrained or has become invisible. They may at first be incapable of 'languaging' important elements of their experience, needing to be respectfully empowered by the counsellor to build up a new story from small successes. They can begin to take part in externalising conversations and list the areas of life where 'the problem' is in charge and the areas where they themselves are in charge. Depression is seldom a clear-cut matter and clients may be in grief or saddened by some event/circumstance, or they may be abusing some substance, or a combination of such factors:

Mary, aged 65, lived alone and was a patient at a GP practice/health centre which had a counsellor. Mary had coped with life until her husband died from an alcohol-related disease. It was known that while her husband was alive Mary also drank a good deal but it did not seem to adversely affect her. After his death, however, she drank to excess, neglecting to eat sufficiently or to care for herself. There were also some incidents of minor self-harm. The doctor had diagnosed depression, linked possibly to grief and had requested that social services provide home support and meals-on-wheels. Even though these services were in place Mary was not making progress, and over a period of several months she was admitted to hospital, stabilised, returned home and admitted again after a few weeks. She was still drinking large quantities of whisky. By the time Mary was referred to the counsellor several professionals were involved and, after working with her on three admissions, the hospital consultant commented to the counsellor that it looked as if 'we are going to lose her'.

The counsellor visited Mary at home, daily at first, encouraging her to tell the story of her life, her husband and her loss. During several hours of listening and validating Mary's experiences the counsellor built up a picture of her strengths and began to be solution-focused. She explored what was different in Mary's life when she was not drinking. Mary talked of how she was more busy and talking to neighbours at those times. Following a scaled question about how well she was coping, she said she was at 3. There was a discussion about what she will be doing when she is at 4, which included visiting the day-centre that people had been talking about and where she could meet some old friends. She still cried over her husband at times and this was seen as normal grief. The counsellor waited until Mary was ready for more future-orientated discussion. When asked a scaled question about her motivation to change, Mary put herself at 5 and when she was asked what she needed to do to move up one step more she was able to describe this clearly.

It was only at this point that the counsellor introduced the 'miracle question'. Mary responded by talking of how she will be smiling like she used to, getting up at a reasonable time, looking forward to keeping her house nice and having a laugh with the next-door neighbour. She was complimented on her strengths and asked what else she will be doing, so that a detailed picture emerged of life after the solution, when drink would be brought under control and she would be caring for herself.

At the next meeting the counsellor felt that Mary had reached the point of belief in her ability to control her drinking, improve the quality of her life further still, free of depression. Over the next few weeks Mary went from strength to strength and was enjoying life.

This example could just as well have exemplified work with alcohol abuse, or work with grief, or work with an older person. We do not believe it is necessary to hypothesise over which difficulty is the greater in a client's life. What is fundamental is a belief in that person's capacity to overcome it once a 'video description' of their own solution is formed and they cease to be identified with, or 'totalised' *as*, the problem.

In conclusion, in this chapter we have used diagnostic terms such as depression, anorexia and psychosis, but we need to stress that in working *with* clients we strive to avoid all such terms. White says that many professional ways of talking produce a subject/object dualism that leads to marginalisation and, indeed, as yet there is no effective challenge to the hegemony of pathologising discourses. Because of the power of language, perhaps it is a useful rule never to use a diagnostic term unless the client uses it first (Simon, SFT e-mail list, 2000). We can also talk of medication not as a *treatment* for a disease but as a means of *facilitating* getting to certain goals (Caron, SFT e-mail list, 1998). If we remain with traditional psychiatric language we risk being responsible for (re)producing the conditions for the very problems we are faced with. A change of words can be the key to the 'liberation' of many clients. As Brian Friel's character, in his play *Translations*, proclaims 'Words are the armoury of the dispossessed'.

9

Happiness, leisure and recreation

Leisure is viewed by most people as a desirable goal in itself but 'having' leisure can be problematic because it ties expectations of happiness and contentment with a negative goal – *not* being occupied by work. How then do people 'do' leisure? How is the free time at their disposal to be filled? Unsatisfactorily-filled leisure is a frequent complaint of clients; albeit often implicit in complaints of feeling generally unhappy because of boredom or lack of friends, partners or a social community of any kind. We get the impression that what some might call 'depression' often seems to have a high boredom content. Some suffer the pain of loss, or of unrequited love, and some may complain of 'loneliness'. Others cope with the boredom of leisure and the pursuit of happiness through the use of 'leisure drugs'. This leads to excesses, addiction or loss of control, which may include criminal activity to fund a craving. The cravings are varied, including a range of 'soft' and 'hard' drugs, alcohol, tobacco – or just shopping or spending. Leisure-without-boredom is a complex construction; leisure-with-contentment/happiness is not easy to construct as many clients will see it as the absence of something, rather than the presence of something, or the *doing* of something specific.

While some aspects of happiness in relationships were discussed in Chapter 6, we will address these aspects of life further in this chapter, focusing more on loss and the pursuit of happiness through substance abuse, drawing on examples from practice. While the practice is easy to describe, the themes in this chapter raise tricky philosophical questions of definition(s), such as 'happiness' or 'addiction'. As with other definitions in this book, we define happiness not as a noun but as a verb. It is *doing* happiness – doing what one does when one feels happy (enough?). Perhaps in our current consumerist society, with its pressures of competition, being 'happy' is not good enough – life has to be 'brill'? For people who have never recognised happiness, for example those who have been abused from a very early age, the relative calm of recovery can seem dull and boring after the adrenaline rush of coping with the abuse and the attention that accompanies disclosure.

So in our practice the definition of realistic attainable goals may take some time. We start by respecting the client's goal even if it is stated as, 'I want to be happy', and we follow the usual clarifying routine of asking how the person will know, what will be different, what they will be doing. If the reply is phrased negatively; for example, 'I will not be home alone', we ask what will be happening *instead*: 'what will you be doing differently when you are not home alone?' Happiness, like sleep, is a 'spontaneous' state to the extent that the harder we try to get it, the further away or the more difficult to achieve it can become. Therefore the solution often entails doing something different to disrupt or change the unsuccessful pattern.

We invent 'happiness scales' such as, '100 means perfect happiness and 1 means how you were when you first arrived here'. Such scales help people to see that there are degrees of problem and degrees of success; difficult aspects are put in context and solutions may sometimes be happening, which the scales help identify. For example, Alex rated himself at 30 on a 'liking himself' scale because he could identify things about himself that he was proud of, but only 20–25 on a 'happiness' scale. He was asked what he would be doing differently if he was a little higher on this scale and replied that he didn't know because he worked nights. His suggested task was to look out for happiness to see if he could spot it coming and what it was like. This was a completely new idea for him and he came to the next session with clear ideas about how he would do happiness, largely concerned with fulfilling previously thwarted abilities. This discovery had clarified what his preferred future would look like.

Loneliness, love and friendship

Happiness is elusive for some people because they have unsatisfactory friendships. Young women, particularly, often tell us that they have been let down by friends who haven't 'been there' for them in times of trouble. We involve these clients in detailed conversations about the meanings of friendship for them and used to ask them to differentiate between supportive and unsupportive friends until Janey came up with a much better explanation: 'Oh', she said, 'you mean silver friends. Like those you just go out with for a good time'. Building on her ideas, we now ask clients to list their gold friends (those with whom they have intimate ties and who can be depended upon always); silver friends (those with whom they can have a laugh but not have high expectations of their reliability); and bronze friends (reliable friends but not necessarily people they see frequently or with whom they have close emotional ties). The subsequent list forms a useful basis for discussions about who is important in the client's life; especially when a 'resent' category is added – they move people into different categories, make decisions about which ones to let go completely and which to treasure. Not expecting the same level of commitment from all friends adds greatly to satisfaction in social relationships.

Unrequited love is a particular form of unhappiness for some people and we have found narratives and metaphors particularly useful in responding to it. Poetry in particular seems to help express not only the problem but possible solutions. We present two metaphors that we have drawn on in our work. The first describes unrequited love as a storm; strong and beautiful but potentially destructive. Therefore one needs to find a safe place to take shelter – perhaps an imaginary cave where there is quiet calm and where one can breathe slowly and quietly, listening to the still small voice of calm as the storm rages past. We talk of a woman who did this each day until gradually her calmness and control grew stronger and the storm became weaker.

The second uses a metaphor of imprisonment and setting free; love can be like a prison, or handcuffs, but we have the power to open the locks, open our arms, and set the other person free, as in the seventeenth-century poem by H. King (1592–1669):

> Let me unfold my arms – let go my fruitless loves,
> that must new fortunes try, like turtle doves
> dislodged from their haunts. I will in tears
> unwind a love knit up in many years.
> With this blown kiss I here surrender thee
> back to thyself, so thou again art free.

There can be a conversation as to whether giving the other person their freedom is the ultimate test of love and/or a conversation about how the client will be when they are free of preoccupation with the other person; for example, see the following extract from a letter written in reply to a client who complained bitterly about being let down by a loved one whom she could not get out of her mind; lack of support from friends; and living a life of superficial happiness:

> I have little to offer you on your strong but ambivalent feelings for him, but I can offer some suggestions for dealing with the intrusive thoughts as I see lots of people who suffer from unrequited love. These are some of the ways they have coped with it:
>
> 1 Make a Valentine box over a period of time; putting in mementos, photographs, tickets and programmes from outings, perhaps even a poem or a letter too. Indulge yourself over this task – remembering both the good and sad times together. When it is complete, put it away and start a new relationship. This has worked really well for people who not only couldn't get the person out of their minds but also found it spoiling new relationships.
>
> 2 Write down *every* single thought about him in an 'obsession' book. This seems to work on the principle that you will soon get fed up as it can become a time-consuming task.
>
> 3 Pin up the H. King poem (enclosed) in a prominent place. It doesn't make letting the person go that much easier, but knowing people have been suffering the same torment since at least the seventeenth century is oddly comforting.
>
> 4 Enlist your friends' help with the sort of support they *can* give. For example, say you are feeling a bit sad about it and can they cheer you up – or join you in a 'blues' night. Don't ask for advice – having these sorts of feelings is still a puzzle to all of us so they won't be able to help out there.
>
> 5 Ring him up and go out with him but do not ask him about the 'offence'. If he doesn't want to talk about something, that's his right and I have never found that it helps in the least to know 'why'. It doesn't take you forward, leads to recriminations and problem talk, and gets in the way of the possibility that you both still have a lot of loving feelings for each other. All you can reasonably ask him is not to lie to you in future.

Or you may have a better idea of your own. If you do have any ideas on how to handle it, give them a try. If they don't work, do something different. Don't forget that there's nothing wrong with what you refer to as 'superficial' happiness – it's *all* happiness. The more you get of the 'superficial' type, the more happiness you will get.

Unhappiness through grief and loss

People who come for grief counselling are often referred by others. Because we do not see grief itself as a problem, we like to ask at some point (after they have told their story and usually done some crying), what the referrer hoped they would get from counselling. We ask if they agree with the referrer; if they do and it is a reasonable goal, we will work with them on it. Grief is a natural response to loss and the form it takes can be greatly influenced by culture. We see it as healthy so long as it is worked through at the person's own pace and in their own way. However, in our anaesthetised Western world many of the traditional supports such as rituals and customs seem to be dying out and displays of grief are seen as embarrassing in some areas, so perhaps what some people need is help *to* grieve. Increasingly people feel that they need to turn to counsellors or doctors for help in coping with grief. This is fine so long as the help does not lead to grieving being stopped or blocked in some way, as can happen if too much medication is used. Ordinary grief should not be seen as a problem, only stuck grief. This is not to say that grief ends at some point – we doubt if it ever completely ends – but it usually reduces to sad memories at specific times such as anniversaries. As it is not always the loss of a person that is causing the grief, it is important to ask future-oriented questions as the example of Margot demonstrates:

Margot referred herself after failing to find help over the past year from a number of voluntary agencies and contacts complaining that she was at the end of her tether. She and her two pre-school children were living with her mother following the death of her husband. She had been married 19 years but her marriage had become 'difficult' and she was considering leaving her husband before he developed cancer and was given six months to live. He lived for three years, during which he became more 'difficult', refusing to go to the hospice even to give her respite. Then his parents arrived from the south to help with him but, to Margot, they were also very difficult; so much so that she moved to her mother's home. Then they would not allow her back to visit her husband and they and her husband moved back south before he died, locked her out of the house, took the contents with them, sold the house. She had to fight to get her share of the equity. Margot felt very bitter about her experiences and could not let the bitterness go. The counsellor acknowledged her feelings and then asked if she wanted to let go of them. She agreed that these feelings of bitterness, anger and resentment were holding her back and she wanted to be able to live her life again. It was all making her very depressed.

The counsellor asked the 'miracle question'; Margot said that what would be different would be that she would have a job and some friends.

Counsellor: What will that help you to do?
Margot: Earn a wage, have more in my pocket, have people to talk to.
Counsellor: Anything else?
Margot: Feel more independent.
Counsellor: What else?
Margot: Get my own place and be livelier with the children.

This line of questioning continued to develop a clear picture of her future hopes but Margot pointed out that her self-esteem was so low that she would never succeed in getting a job and neither could she cope with a full-time job. She raised the possibility of voluntary work or evening classes to develop interests and confidence, then returned to her depression, for which she is taking medication.

Counsellor: On a scale of 0 to 10, with 0 meaning the pits, where are you today?
Margot: About 2, heading for 1.
Counsellor: What will be happening, that's not happening now, that will tell you that you have moved up to 3?
Margot: Getting out a bit more.
Counsellor: Do you get out sometimes now?
Margot: Occasionally, I walk to the shops.
Counsellor: I am interested in hearing that you walk to the shops – I have heard of someone who walked out of 'depressoland' [a term coined by O'Hanlon] by starting with a daily walk to the shops for a newspaper. She got up early, dressed, put on some make-up etc. On returning from the shop she had a coffee. In this way she had better days and she went on to walk herself out of the problem in other ways too.
Margot: And I could write in my diary what I do each day.
Counsellor: Noting when you feel better might also be useful.

At the next session, the counsellor noticed that Margot was looking much brighter and asked what was better.

Margot: I feel now that I can tell you about my friend, a man I met some time ago and who wants to be a friend. I have been unlucky with two marriages. The first lasted only six months – he was violent. I still feel very angry towards my last in-laws but I know I can get on with my life.

Counsellor: How else have things been better since we met?

Margot: Well, I have done something every day to keep going and I have written it in my diary. [She listed the tasks, including a daily walk and she was obviously pleased with herself. The children seemed calmer and she was coping better with them, with some help from her mother.] I must let go of what they did and start living.

Counsellor: On a scale of 0 to 10, 10 being high, how confident are you that you can do that?

Margot: 7. I've just realised that I've not taken my tablets this morning. I just didn't need them, I suppose.

Rest, relaxation and sleep

Rest, relaxation and sleep are important aspects of leisure or 're-creation'. Lack of sleep concerns many clients and, here again, we have found brief-counselling approaches useful. Solution-focused approaches have been found to be helpful in helping those who have difficulty in falling asleep or in getting enough sleep; see, for example, de Shazer's training video (de Shazer, 1997), which demonstrates his 'radical acceptance' of the client's view as a way of developing a helpful engagement which enables the client to discover her own ingenious solution to her difficulty. Sleep, like happiness, is a spontaneous activity which can't 'happen' if a person is trying to make it happen but, as in any situation involving spontaneity or randomness, prediction tasks can help clients locate aspects of control in difficulties that at first seem beyond their control. They also disrupt failing patterns of 'trying too hard'. The more clients practise predicting 'good' nights, the more they are likely to get better at predicting accurately. If they can predict an event, they have some measure of control or influence over it.

The narrative approach, too, has been useful to us in work with this issue. Because sleep disturbance, like most other difficulties, is often linked or combined with other problems such as trauma or anxiety, the narrative can vary widely. Children may fear monsters in the dark; adults may fear terrifying memories or threats of violence. Anything that helps people to cope better with these will also help with sleep. For example, nine-year-old Leonie has always been a fearful child but a burglary increased her fearfulness to the extent that she was unable to sleep in her own bed at night or play in her bedroom unless other family members were upstairs. Her parents and younger sister, Bryony, were so short of sleep that they were losing patience with her. Small improvements resulted from a search for exceptions but her progress became more rapid after her problem was externalised as Problem Panic, and she identified her form teacher as a person with expertise in this sort of problem; see the following extract from notes made after her third session:

PROBLEM

Leonie still has some fear, worry and panic but it is not as bad as it was. It looks as though the main problem is that Problem Panic has crept into Leonie's life on the back of ordinary panic about the burglary and has been stopping Leonie doing the thing she likes by making her think that she is worried all the time.

PROGRESS/EXCEPTIONS

1 Mum says that Leonie has been much better this week. She has been going into her bedroom to fetch things, sleeping on a mattress in mum and dad's room (this has helped a lot), and not always getting into mum and dad's bed. Everyone is getting more sleep. This shows as both Leonie and her mum were looking smart and pretty when they came for the appointment.

2 Grandma says that Leonie is much calmer; not following her upstairs or ringing up about worry.

3 Leonie is getting to understand panic. It has a medium shape because she doesn't feel sad when she is at grandma's. Leonie also knows that Problem Panic has been tricking her into being a little kid; like Bryony having to look after Leonie instead of the other way round, getting Leonie to cry, need company all the time, and be snappy with people. Problem Panic also might have been working through grandma because it is a grandma's job to spoil children.

THOUGHTS ON SOLUTIONS

1 Leonie thought out a list of questions and then interviewed her form teacher. She has written the questions and answers down and filed them in a Recovery From Problem Panic Folder. Her teacher knows a lot of girls who have had similar fears to Leonie (including herself) and has some good ideas about how to handle them. She suggested talking about the fears, keeping a diary so that Leonie can notice small changes, and a chart to see if some days are better. Leonie has done all these things. Her chart shows three smiley faces, five all right faces, and only two sad faces. The folder is super.

2 Leonie has some ideas of her own for stopping Problem Panic pushing her around. She will go to her room for some short times and talk back at it. She will say 'no, no' (she is good at saying 'no'), or 'I am doing something else'. Leonie also thinks she can be in her own room if Bryony is in her bedroom.

3 It turns out that Leonie's imaginary friend is called P. Fred. This is absolutely the best name for an imaginary friend who is going to help Leonie with Problem Panic.

HOMEWORK

1 More of the same because Leonie has made tremendous progress.

2 Leonie might toss an Italian coin (she had a very happy holiday in Italy). If the coin comes up on the happy side, she will pretend all day that she is brave, strong and happy to see if this tricks Problem Panic. If the coin comes up on the other side, she will have an ordinary day. She will not tell her mum and dad which side the coin comes up. They will notice how she is and try to work out which day is which.

3 Leonie might make a dream catcher for her room. She has some good ideas about what this will look like. It might have an Italian coin to remind her of happy times, a little book (Leonie is good at reading), and a photograph of her auntie when she won a prize for dancing (Leonie hopes to be a dancer when she grows up).

We find that children and young women often find a dream catcher useful to handle fear which is associated with the bedroom, especially when they are individually designed. The hoop and mesh can be of any colour and fabric which the client chooses and we suggest adding symbols representing hopes, achievements and aspirations. The conversation about these items is therapeutic in itself. For example, Fiona's symbol of a time when she felt both happy and secure was a pink sunset over a lake and talking about how this could be incorporated into her dream catcher reminded her of previous coping strategies for bad nights – a jug of water at the bedside helped her 'flush away' bad thoughts and the colour pink was decided on for her redecoration scheme.

Seeking happiness through substance abuse

Many clients seek help in overcoming an addiction, and here again there is a definition problem. We avoid pathological definitions or definitions that undermine accountability or the possibility of accountability; for example, the term 'dependent'. We also try to avoid focusing on 'quitting' as that is a problem focus, where the goal would be the absence of something – a void – rather than the presence of something. A 'quitting' focus also leads to negative ideas like the prevention of relapse (the prevention of failure).

Much has been written on the subject of alcoholism, drug abuse and addiction which is in stark contrast to our approach. Traditionally addiction was seen as a disease and, at least as far as alcohol went, it was seen as an incurable disease. When the Sobells (1978) introduced 'controlled drinking' in the 1960s, there were allegations of 'not understanding the disease', or of 'denial'; people who were able to control their drinking were said not to have been 'real alcoholics'; and because problems built up over years, years of 'deep' therapy were required so rapid progress was dismissed as 'flight into health' (for a fuller discussion, see Berg and Miller, 1992). These ideas still hold sway; for example, the AA's '12-Steps' model holds to the incurability of alcoholism as an inherited disease. All 'alcoholics' are considered to be alike, resistant and 'in denial' and only one outcome is acceptable – total abstinence for life; 'take one drink and the drink will take you'. In this approach the only option on 'hitting bottom' is to 'surrender/admit defeat and give up trying to co-exist with alcohol'. Not only is this a long process, it is a lifelong effort that may also involve costly inpatient treatment and years of outpatient groupwork, leading to an identification of the person with 'being' an alcoholic, repeating at each session, 'I am John and I am an alcoholic'. Family members

are seen as targets too, lest they contribute to maintaining the problem (so-called co-dependence), and groups are set up for them. This
approach has helped some people, partly perhaps because it puts something into a life (AA membership), to replace the drinking.

By the late 1980s, several writers were describing effective forms
of brief counselling of five to six sessions (see, for example, Garfield,
1989; Budman and Gurman, 1988). Wallerstein's study (1989) showed
that those undertaking such short courses did as well as those under-
going long-term extensive treatment. Berg and Miller (1992) and Berg
and Reuss (1998), who use a solution-focused approach and philosophy, suggest that this change of thinking mirrors the change in
counselling or psychotherapy generally.

We recognise that excessive consumption of alcohol leads to grave
social consequences, aggravating crime, violence, family abuse and
neglect. However, notions of 'incurable inherited disease' usually lead
either to a self-fulfilling prophesy or a total denial, which adds to the
trouble – as if things were not bad enough. So while we do not minimise
the harm being done, we have seen that recovery can be as rapid as
the recovery of people from any other difficulty for which they seek
counselling. Many people can control alcohol without total abstinence.
The same applies to drug users: 'Contrary to the traditional view of
these clients as "resistant" to treatment, we found this population pleasant and willing to work with us in solving their unique problems' (Berg
and Miller, 1992: xvii). Like Berg and Miller, we do not claim that
solution-focused or narrative approaches can be successful in all cases,
or that other approaches cannot help, but we doubt if there is such a
thing as alcoholism. In our view there are as many 'alcoholisms' as there
are people with drink-related problems: 'or, perhaps more radically, there
are none at all' (de Shazer, 1994: 244).

As with any other problem, we do not feel a need to understand
'cause' in order to be helpful. We may explore how a person was recruited into abusing alcohol or other drugs, what restrained them from
being in control, what social or family lies did they hear, and have
they ever been able to resist these – the unique outcomes. Solution-
focused workers seek out exceptions: 'The primary focus is on the
successes of clients in dealing with their problems' (Berg and Miller,
1992: 3). Strengths and abilities are discussed, not deficits and failures; the focus being not on pathology but on the preservation and
promotion of health. The belief is that clients have the solutions already
and need only to be helped to recognise them; for instance, those

occasions when they are able to do something different to create exceptions. The intervention is about putting these differences to work to make a difference in the person's life, utilising the client's own abilities and unrecognised solutions. Berg and Miller believe that so-called resistant clients are people who are unable to cooperate with counsellors *who do not co-operate with them* by listening carefully to what they want. Resistance is natural if one is being forced to do what one does not want. The counsellor needs to consider whether the client wants help to control or end his or her own drinking. Sometimes the client is complaining about someone else's drinking, in which case we start from there.

Clients will often have a theory of cause, blaming some past experience, person or circumstance for behaviour of which they are frequently ashamed. We listen to these explanations but what we are concerned about is their willingness to accept responsibility for their *future* behaviour and the achievement of their attainable goals. Some will want total abstinence, some will want controlled social drinking, some will be in despair. Berg and Reuss (1998) maintain that solution-focused practice has much in common with the *original* AA and 'The Big Book' (total abstinence and disease theory were introduced only when AA was professionalised later on), so with the first group, we ask if they have experience of the AA. If 'yes', we ask if it was useful and we encourage them to repeat any successes they had. If attending AA was not helpful, we ask what do they think will be helpful instead. With the second group we check out what they want from controlled social drinking as many people tell us that they have a good time when drinking heavily. For example, Jack described 'getting wrecked' with his mates as 'making a right good night of it'. The counsellor asked him how he knew that he was having a good time if he could not remember anything of the later part of the evening. He reported at the next session that he went out on a planned bender with his mates and drank lightly so that he could observe how they were having a good time. He came to the conclusion that 'getting wrecked' did not lead to having a good time and reduced his drinking to two cans of lager.

We have extended this 'experiment' to other forms of substance abuse. Rachel maintained that smoking heroin was enjoyable and that she couldn't refuse it anyway as she smoked with a group of friends. The counsellor asked her to be the last person in the group to smoke and watch the effect it had on her friends. Her observations led her to refuse the opportunity when it came to her turn; made considerably easier by the fact that her friends were too stoned to exert any peer group pressure on her.

The traditional relapse-prevention approach developed by Marlatt and Gordon (1980) also presents problems for us. This approach is based on the so-called 'chronic relapsing nature' of alcoholism, leading to stories of failure after failure in clients with poor coping strategies for situations of high temptation. The approach consists of identifying high-risk situations and gradually exposing the client to them. We see this as focusing on opportunities for *failure* and on ways of *avoiding* failure, in a way that draws attention to the 'forbidden' activity, thereby virtually setting the client up to fail:

> Attempting to stop someone from doing something is much more difficult than building on and enhancing activities that they are already doing . . . rather than focusing on 'high risk' situations, the solution-focused approach focuses on 'high success' situations . . . promoting those situations wherein the client is likely to be the most *successful*. (Berg and Miller, 1992: 129–30, our emphasis).

In any case, how can one say when one has stopped doing anything; it is much easier to say when one has started doing something. If setbacks occur we see them as proof of earlier success – people cannot slip back unless they have moved forward. In any difficult enterprise, setbacks are normal. Clients' perceptions of the process are the most important as people are likely to behave according to their perceptions, perhaps using a graph to show setbacks on a line of overall progress. Janey, for example, reported going out with friends to the pub and 'not getting wrecked' because she didn't want to be hung over the next day on a planned outing with her mum, but added, 'I know I can do it again – if I *want* to'. She had also changed the way she viewed herself:

> I feel better in myself. I don't worry what people think about me now but I take care how I behave when I'm out. When I think what I was like, getting wrecked, staggering round town in the middle of the night, getting upset over people who're not worth it, arguing with my mum. I don't want to be like that again. I feel like I've got my life back. I'm happy.

There was every chance that if she *wanted* to drink soberly with friends she could. Getting their life back, 'getting by', seems to us to be how many people most satisfactorily 'do' happiness. Carr (2000) has an interesting approach to quitting the use of addictive substances. We have commented earlier that 'quitting' is a negative, problem-focused goal, but he combines his educative approach with a narrative idea of two monsters. First he challenges the thinking of the client, questioning the logic of their behaviour by suggesting that the true reason a person uses the substance is to feed the little monster inside – to satisfy the craving. But, he goes on, the drug does not satisfy the craving, it causes it and the satisfaction is only a temporary return to life before the abuse and the craving started. It is only an illusion of pleasure, calming the 'little monster' it has created. In addition there is a 'big monster' to deal with – attitudes and beliefs created in society by alcohol and tobacco companies in particular. These ideas include how boredom and stress are relieved and relaxation and concentration is improved. 'Addiction', he claims, is more mental than physical, and the mental aspect is simply the ideas promoted by the 'big monster' that we cannot enjoy or even cope with life without the substance. A cigarette will even help you to cope with a firing squad! The 'big' social monster paves the way, including lying to young people about not being able to be mature without the stuff, and the 'little monster' 'proves' how necessary it is: 'If you believe that you can't enjoy life or handle stress without a cigarette, you will feel miserable and insecure without one' (Carr, 2000: 31). He talks of the tug of war between two sides of the mind – 'It's a filthy slavery, destroying my health', and 'It's my friend and crutch'. He names this a 'fear', fear of failing to cope without, a fear non-users do not have. The two monsters create the illusion of pleasure or crutch and not using is spoken of as 'giving up'; that is, making a dreadful sacrifice. He reports a 90 per cent success rate with cigarette smokers.

To those in despair about their substance abuse, we can say, 'I can see what a terrible time you have been through and I can understand why you feel hopeless, but I would like to know how you have kept going in spite of this?' The *in spite of* turns the problem into a compliment about strength – the worse the situation the bigger the compliment. Exceptions will emerge with patience. Again the bigger the mess, the more exceptions can be cheered.

Many problem-focused counsellors consider that clients who use hard drugs require referral to specialist clinics, or at least specially trained counsellors who know about drugs. While such knowledge may or may not be useful, we have found that these clients can respond to solution-focused and narrative approaches as well as any other client group, largely because it honours clients' own solutions rather than prescribing a way of quitting. The ingenuity of their solutions never fails to impress us. For example, Maggie had tried every method of quitting suggested by a specialist drugs service before her parents brought her for brief counselling as a last desperate measure. As the whole family came with her, even a brother who had taken time off work in another part of the country, they were asked what family solution would use their obvious strengths. Having seen the film *Trainspotter*, they opted to shadow Maggie for some weeks to support her when she met up with her boyfriend who was still a user. Maggie was delighted about the planned 'imprisonment' which allowed her to withdraw gradually from her boyfriend as well as quickly from heroin. Within two weeks she had obtained a job and started a new life.

Similarly, Colin was becoming increasingly despondent about his failure to comply with a prescribed methadone reduction programme, prior to acceptance for a detoxification place. His preferred solution was to be arrested for his unpaid debts and detox in prison. When he 'failed' to get a prison sentence, he rethought his solutions and abandoned the methadone programme, preferring instead to smoke rather than inject heroin in the intervening period. He was able to detox successfully this way. As mentioned at the end of Chapter 1, our views on expertise honour the 'local' knowledge of clients and we sometimes ask them if they have helpful ideas for other clients who may be experiencing similar difficulties. Colin's solution-finding was a case in point. Seven months after working on his withdrawal from heroin (three sessions in all), Colin called in at the project to say that he had a job overseas. He was consulted on what advice he would give to a young man the counsellor was currently seeing for a similar problem; the conversation was typed up and a copy sent to both men; a brief part of which is outlined below:

Counsellor: I do need some advice though. I'm seeing a lad in prison and he's a lot like you used to be. His problems with his dad aren't quite as bad as your's but, like you, he keeps ending up doing another sentence. It's heroin, and anger, and depression; you know all that — been there, done that. The thing is, he's having a really bad time in prison. For a start, he's come off heroin but he has to sit in his pad with his mate doing heroin in front of him. You managed prison quite well so I wondered if I could pick your brains a bit ...

Colin: If it's [name of prison], it's awash with heroin. I've a mate in there now on the detox unit. Another mate, he got himself sent down so he could make money dealing. He made a couple of grand. He got a mate who was clean to take his visits. They watch your visits if you're a user; so you get someone else to do the transfer...There's plenty of people in prison who don't take it. He should write to the governor stipulating he wants a pad mate who's clean. No. He can't do that, it'd be grassing someone up. What I did was put my pad mate's gear outside the cell and say 'sorry mate, but I don't want to share with a user'. Then *he's* got to ask for a change. Is he strong enough to do this, like what is he like?

Counsellor: He's tough, muscular. Problem is the screws don't like him and move any pad mate he gets on with.

Colin: Tell him [pad mate] you're laughing at him with his habit knowing you've got no dependence on drugs. You don't have to suffer detox like he does.

Counsellor: How do you prevent a slipback?

Colin: I write things down. I write things down all the time, put it on the bedroom wall. Positives and negatives. Negatives – are you doing this to kill time and have to wake up the next morning feeling poorly? Positives – gets you through the day. Negative – you've got to do it again the next day ... it's one day at a time with no days off.

Counsellor: What if you do have a day off?

Colin: Don't worry about slipbacks. Just forget all about them and think 'I'll give it another go'. It gets easier the more you try because you know what's coming. With a heavy user like I was, it only takes four, five days to get hooked again so withdrawal comes more quickly. Like, if you took heroin, it'd take four, maybe five months to get hooked. Me, I can't afford to get myself hooked again. You'd build up like that if you took it regular.

Counsellor: What's the hardest part?

Colin: What's difficult is walking out of your house and seeing someone you spent a lot of time with and they're still doing drugs. You have to ignore them. No. Not ignore them exactly. Not spend any time with them, go anywhere with them. Of my mates, there was about 20 of us, five are dead, five are in jail with big sentences, five or six went to work – that's all, no drugs, and the rest done jail, detoxed and come off. But they had to change their lives and ways of thinking. I'm going to [name of town where he has a job] because of being too near the scene of the crime. Like you're watching *Eastenders* and thinking you used to do heroin when you watched that. So you need a substitute. Take up another interest, reading or improving yourself. Keeping your mind occupied. You draw strength from waking up the next morning feeling all right. You can tell this lad, he wakes up okay but his pad mate wakes up sweating. And he has to worry about getting a good kicking. When you're clean you don't have no pressures because you owe someone a tenner.

Counsellor: How did you control your anger when you were in prison?

Colin: If I'm controlling my anger, I use it in a more positive way. By counting to ten. Daft as it sounds, it works. Sit there on a night and write down thoughts and feelings. I do a lot of thinking on positives and negatives: am I happy with what I'm doing with my time now? Ask myself, am I happy? What would make me feel better? If I answer heroin, ask myself for how long? I can let you have what I've written if you like.

These ideas were shared with a client who was in prison. The relayed conversation was helpful to him in that it offered him *credible* practical advice and hope; to Colin because it strengthened his new story; and to the counsellor, who gained valuable 'local knowledge'. It demonstrates that while there is no such thing as a typical or ordinary person, there are many people with previously untapped abilities, courage and tenacity. Identifying these qualities is of vital importance in effective counselling.

In conclusion, when leisure is socially constructed as a non-activity, it has little potential to add to personal happiness. Even where a client is so worn out with unreasonable and unachievable responsibilities and hardships as to need a complete rest, relaxation can be hard to come by – as witnessed by so many clients finding what should be a gentle wind-down before sleep the most problematic period of the day; a time when intrusive thoughts disturb their peace. Neither does leisure *per se* offer the potential to tap the creativity of clients; indeed, Reeves (2001) argues that happiness is to be found within the workplace, which has become our community – a place where we meet friends and fall in love, and where we gain a sense of identity and self-worth. Rather we consider *recreation* a more useful term to use in our conversations with clients. Recreation implies *activity*; of a person being agreeably occupied, being creative, and regenerating themselves. And recreation is not bound by restrictive ideas on how it must be done, being sufficiently broad a term to encompass both intensely absorbing individual pursuits and pleasant social activities.

Although we may not be sure how to use 'leisure', we do know that we all 'do' recreation differently – depending largely on discovering how we 'do' happiness. Judith, reared in the industrial north of England to a Protestant work ethic, is attracted to the ideas of Schiller, in his 'Essay on the Connection between the Physical and Spiritual Nature of Man' (Garland, 1976), that happiness comes from having *just* more purposeful activity than one has time to do. Thus work and leisure are inextricably linked and a reasonable amount of stress is pleasurable. Patrick, reared as a Catholic in rural Ireland to a more reflective ethic, is attracted to the ideas of de Milo (1990) that happiness is internal; to acquire it we do not have to do anything because it cannot be *acquired,* since we already have it. He maintains that we may not experience it at times because we let illusions, greed or cravings get in the way; once we recognise these and externalise them, we can drop unhappiness without needing to try to change reality; looking for external excitement or thrills leads only to feeling miserable and dissatisfied. But perhaps Patrick's happiness involves doing a little more than just thinking this way.

These two examples of doing happiness show how it is related to culture. In counselling therefore, cultural, religious and racial differences, where notions of happiness may not have imported the ideas of an authentic or fulfilled self, need to be respected. Having a goal seems to be central to 'doing' happiness but there are as many different goals as there are people.

10

Conclusion

Our philosophical assumptions

First we believe people have what it takes to get what they want; this potential just needs to be brought into consciousness and mobilised. Clients already know how to deal adequately with their problems although they may need help to realise this. We convey our belief that they are competent and this compliment makes their abilities more available to them. We therefore utilise everything that a person brings to a session, drawing on any talent that is identified no matter how irrelevant it may seem; and by patient questions help them to talk themselves into making changes, for only they know what a satisfying life will be like for them. These changes are rarely the ones we would have recommended had we viewed ourselves as experts, so the process can seem slow and laborious in the initial stages as we seek the minutest details of clients' competencies.

We accept the social constructionist theory that talking together about what a solution will look like, using 'video talk' to picture the new story in all its aspects, helps to create it and make it 'real', greatly enhancing the possibility of it happening. Films, like most good stories, include action, dialogue, location and emotions; so the conversation can be not only about what is happening and what individuals are doing, but also about what they are saying, what is the location like, and what feelings are being generated as the new plot thickens.

Our disinterest in finding causes is based on a fear that any so-called cause will probably lead to a label or a pathology, and also a belief that if there is a cause it is no more than one narrative construct:

Therapy, like politics, has always rested on the construction and maintenance of social reality. Until recently, therapists practised in accordance with

169

a set of enduring and given 'truths'. Unfortunately, these 'truths' acted to conceal and support monopolistic ambitions to control information on what constitutes right and wrong, normal and abnormal. (Epston, 1998: 128)

While structuralists seek out the deep structures that underlie problems, constructionists prefer to stay on the surface. Troubles are not considered to be deeply buried, rather that solutions are difficult to see because they are under our noses. Staying on the surface also prevents us from taking expertise away from clients. They are the surface experts; expert on what is happening and what needs to happen. Our only expertise is in asking useful questions, studiously avoiding pathologising, and making our own values transparent as we do subscribe wholeheartedly to some dominant narratives:

I believe there are some times when totalisation is necessary. It would be self-indulgent and morally unacceptable not to support the anti-racist forces that are attempting to unite black people, and a white person has no right to tell black people how to organise their resistance. However I believe that solidarity with anti-racism should not be equated to a non-critical and knee-jerk acceptance of . . . anti-discriminatory orthodoxy. (Katz, 1996: 213)

We resist the traditional tendency to hash over problems and assign pathological significance; although if a *client* finds talking about them helpful, then they are recommended to do more of it. We accept that trouble has happened, moving on to seek an understanding of solutions in the future. The exciting part is that, to a greater or lesser extent, we never know for certain what problem is being solved until the solution has been found. We treat clients' concerns, language, experiences and views as sensible and adequate, and we are committed to parsimony, using minimal interventions and getting out of people's lives as quickly as possible.

We have a fundamental distrust of science as privileged knowledge of 'facts'. We have more respect for the 'local' knowledges and constructions which are,

linked to the circumstance in which they are produced . . . narratives that make sense in particular social, cultural and historical circumstances but not necessarily generalisable [for] all knowledge is contingent on diverse local circumstances associated with its use. (Miller, 1997: 63)

We try to avoid generating hypotheses based on general theories, although it is difficult to tear oneself away from one's training in them. Following no general explanatory or normative model enables us to turn to clients and their unique ideas instead. We are 'radically particularistic' in our orientation towards people's troubles and our own intervention, seeking out the unique possibilities in each situation but not searching for one single correct solution – we assume there are many.

In our approach, the Western assumption that language is a neutral medium for conveying ideas is challenged. Instead language is seen as generative of realities that are sustained by it; these 'realities' and meanings are constantly shifting and contingent on context and on 'language games'; although we remind ourselves constantly that language itself is essentially man-made (Graddol and Swann, 1989; Spender, 1985). Problems and solutions are seen as different language games that need not be related. We prefer to not define problems, and we have even found that it is possible to help solve a problem without knowing what it actually is. We are, however, intensely interested in the relationships people have with their problems and how they would like to change this relationship. The approach is essentially affirmative and optimistic, seeing many reasons why clients can be confident about their future lives. While we will make value-based decisions on our own when necessary for the safety of clients, we prefer to be collaborative with clients.

As for responsibility, we see ourselves as individually responsible for building clients' confidence and self-agency and jointly responsible with our clients for constructing solutions. Clients are not blamed for their problems, but they are held responsible for working on change with us. We are responsible for ensuring the client is given 'a voice in determining the course of their lives' (Berg, 1994: 61). We are also responsible for acknowledging pain and frustration, and structural inequalities; for reminding people that change can be hard work; and for moving the narrative on to 'progressive' tracks if necessary.

Brief counselling has been described as 'a language game', not in the sense that we play games with people's difficulties, but we seek to use the language of the client to create with them something new. The term 'game' reminds us that we are talking about practices, not essences or even explanations. We are aware that language has game-like rules. Miller (1997) describes this work as 'serious play'. Life is seen as an ongoing narrative project in which we are all responsible storytellers. The process is collaborative, designed to show clients how to take responsibility for their narratives . . . to persuade clients to accept responsibility by developing new life stories perhaps developing a less serious orientation to the 'small stuff' of everyday life. (Miller 1997: 215)

This subverts the Western assumption that our lives are full of 'facts' over which we have limited control; when faced with problematic 'facts' we can change the story. This does not mean wishing problems out of existence, but rather experiencing them differently; what Spacks (1986) refers to as the subversive effect of 'serious gossip'. Our choices in life are shaped by the meanings we give to events for, as a species, we have evolved to use mental narratives to organise, understand and predict our lived experiences, including their many contradictions. The line between knowing what is, and interpreting what is, is more blurred than has been supposed, for it is the words that construct the experience of what is: 'Gossip's way of telling can project a different understanding of reality from that of society at large . . . gossip epitomizes a way of knowing as well as telling' (Spacks, 1986: 46).

In our practice we talk with people from an assumption that we are all normal and competent, therefore the practice techniques are rooted in that assumption and the other philosophical assumptions outlined above. The practice is essentially ways of developing a clear picture of the goal – the future without the problem – described in all its interactional detail, together with developing motivation and confidence in one's ability through scaled questions, co-constructing a self-made future for which clients take only that responsibility which is both reasonable and achievable.

Does it work?

In enthusiastically espousing solution talk as our preferred approach to counselling we must also explain why we recommend that counsellors trained in other approaches might give it serious consideration. While all research findings demonstrate that other forms of brief counselling, particularly cognitive approaches, are not only effective but well-liked by clients (see, for example, Culley and Wright, 1997; Buchanan, 1999; Chapman and Hough, 2001) we offer the following reasons for our preference:

- All therapy models work to some extent but outcome research shows that solution-focused and narrative approaches have the potential to cater for a very much wider range of clients than usual, particularly poor people with significant problems; they are more economical in terms of the number of sessions needed; and have a lower drop-out rate (see Appendix 1 for details of these studies). Clients with long-standing problems are less likely to do well, requiring further follow-up sessions when they develop new problems (see, for example, Macdonald, 1997), although our experience of failure seems to be with clients who have long standing problems and low motivation to change. Hopelessness and poorly-defined goals do not present obstacles, but we do find it difficult to move clients onto a progressive narrative when they are persistently unable to answer questions such as 'how will you know when you don't need to come for counselling anymore', or are unable to 'take a step in a direction that will be good for you'. Veterans of counselling who cannot envisage life without counselling constitute our biggest failures. They are not cited in this book simply because they have not given us their permission.

- Our drop-out rate is satisfyingly low. For example, although for clients referring themselves to our newly-formed domestic violence programme (which caters for both heterosexual and same-sex violence) the drop-out between making the first appointment and attending is roughly one-third, the same as other programmes (see, for example, Burton *et al.*, 1989), we have had a 100 per cent completion rate once people attend the first session. This is particularly gratifying as the research suggests that self-referral drop-out rates vary between 50–73 per cent (Burton *et al.*, 1989; Dobash *et al.*, 2000). This is our best result with what is as yet a small number of clients, and our overall drop-out rate is in the region of 5 per cent; although we subsequently find that some drop-outs write months later to tell us that they are doing well. For example, Carmel sent a Christmas card to us saying: 'Sorry I haven't been in touch. I'm doing OK with the help of my husband and family. Life goes on! I changed my job and feel a lot happier. I've put most of the past in the box we were talking about. Thanks for caring.'

- Clients express high levels of satisfaction with the approach taken. This is not only in terms of outcomes but also the process. Solution-focused approaches are often criticised for their seemingly formulaic approach and their comparative disinterest in feelings and emotions;

a common complaint we get at training sessions is that the approach is surely unsuitable for people who are suffering bereavement. Yet we find, like Turnell and Lipchik (1999), that clients tell us they experienced being understood at the deepest of levels. For example, Sarah's experiences of loss due to the death of her first child and a subsequent post-natal depression were not specifically addressed; the counsellor concentrating instead on Sarah's preferred future. When asked at the fourth (and final session) what had been most helpful, Sarah replied: 'Not being guided by you, just acknowledging how devastating bereavement has been on all planes of my life. It was really bad but you never brushed it aside. Life will never be the same again but you can be happy.' In reaching her goals, Sarah has come to terms with her sadness and grief.

- A huge bonus from using an approach which focuses on strengths and the discovery of solutions is that the client knows we are interested in happiness rather more than misery. This has two advantages over other approaches. First the sessions are more fun. Hannah had serious problems but replied to the questions at the end of the first session about her expectations and suggestions for how the counsellor could be more helpful: 'It wasn't at all what I expected. I enjoyed it. When I saw my last counsellor, I used to come in feeling all right and then we talked about my problems and I was in tears by the time I came out.' We wonder how miserable the counsellor felt at the end of each session too. Second, letters and cards, often months and years later, confirm for us the long-lasting effects of a counselling approach that is often criticised for being a superficial and encouraging 'flight into health'. Macdonald's research (1997) also challenges such notions.

    These are extracts from a letter that Sadie sent to us: 'As you may remember I went away to Hopton school and it was the best thing that ever happened to me. I came home for the summer and found an old shoe box with some notes and letters in it. I found my old diary and your letter. That's when I thought I would write and tell you how I am getting on with my life . . . I have been at Hopton two years and achieved a great deal . . . I also found a new talent (well sort of, I need a bit more confidence yet) but I started singing and a month ago I did my first solo. . . . I auditioned for Hopton senior college and got it, as well as a grant for the next three years. . . . You showed me that I need to plan my action in a way that suits me, what I can do best, and carry it out with minimum fuss. You taught me to have confidence and bravery. I still think now, when I need to stick up for myself, about "debating skills". . . . I hope you pass this on the people it helps. It's a nice feeling knowing that you can make a difference to someone's life like you did with mine . . . tell them, even though they may feel there is no way out, there is. I found it and I feel like a human again. My friends 'take the mickey' because I smile all the time. They have no idea that I smile because I'm happy because I have my life back . . .'

- Most of all, we enjoy the freedom from worry that our surrender of expertise leads to. To paraphrase Wingarten (1998), we don't know 'truths' about people's lives and it is great no longer to believe that we must know. Because we have no hidden expertise, we rarely get into conflictual relationships with our clients – a feature of high drop-out rates (Beyebach and Carranza, 1997). As resistance is viewed more as 'discontent with the agenda' (Furman and Ahola, 1992), we simply seek the client's unique way of cooperating and ask more questions. This means that we are not burnt out with the burden of expertise, seemingly non-cooperative clients, or attempting to manage risk. The approach not only aims to help clients lead more joyous lives, it has a therapeutic effect on the counsellor too. All this encourages us to be more creative and continue learning from our clients.

A last word. As our philosophy is 'if it works do more of it, if it doesn't work, do something different,' we suggest that if your approach works for you, if both you and your clients are happy with both the product and process, then ignore our enthusiasm. Do more of what you are already doing. If you are less happy, we invite you to discover your possibilities by using solution talk the next time you feel frustrated at the lack of progress one of your clients is making. Realising, however, that the approach *sounds* easy, we emphasise that while it may be simple to *understand*, it is still hard to keep to the discipline.

Appendix 1 Some outcome studies

Our position on outcomes is that we owe it to clients to offer the best possible service; the crucial test being effectiveness. Solution-focused and narrative counselling seeks, therefore, to establish whether it is as effective as other approaches and to this end numerous evaluation studies have been undertaken, a selection of which is listed below:

Besa, D. (1994) 'Evaluating Narrative Therapy using Single-System Research Designs', *Research on Social Work Practice*, 4 (3): 309–25. This study evaluated narrative-based family work with six families. In five families the improvement in child-parent relationships varied from 88 per cent to 98 per cent.
Beyebach, M., Morejan, A.R., Palenzuela, D.L. and Rodriguez-Arais, J.L. (1996) 'Research on the Process of Solution Focused Therapy' in *Handbook of Solution Focused Brief Therapy* (eds) S.D. Miller, M.A. Hubble and B.L. Duncan (San Francisco: Jossey-Bass). Of 39 outpatients in a mental-health setting, 80 per cent achieved their goals in an average of five sessions.
Burr, W. (1993) 'Evaluation of the Use of Brief Therapy in a Practice for Children and Young People', *Familiendynamik*, 18: 11–21. 55 cases were followed up and of the 34 replies, 77 per cent reported significant improvement.
Jong, P. and Hopwood, L.E. (1996) 'Outcome Research on Treatment Conducted at the Brief Family Therapy Centre 1992–1993', in *Handbook of Solution Focused Brief Therapy* (eds) S.D. Miller, M.A. Hubble and B.L. Duncan (San Francisco: Jossey-Bass). Of 275 clients 45 per cent achieved their goals and a further 32 per cent made significant progress in an average of 2.9 sessions.
De Shazer, S. (1985) *Keys to Solutions in Brief Therapy* (New York: Norton), pp. 147–57. Follow-up of 28 clients showed that 82 per cent not only met their goals in an average of five sessions, but solved other problems too.
De Shazer, S. (1991) *Putting Difference to Work* (New York: Norton), pp. 161–2). Follow-up on 23 clients showed that 80 per cent either resolved their original difficulty or made significant progress resolving it in four sessions. At later follow-up (18 months) the success rate increased to 86 per cent.
Eakes, G., Walsh, S., Markowski', M., Cain, H. and Swanson, M. (1997) 'Family-centred Brief Solution Focused Therapy with Chronic Schizophrenia: A Pilot Study', *Journal of Family Therapy*, 19: 145–58. This reports the results of 5 sessions of solution-focused work combined with narrative work over 10 weeks with families with a member diagnosed as schizophrenic compared with a control group who received problem-focused work. The experimental group increased their self-agency whilst the control group depended more on medication.

Fisher, D.J., Himble, J.A. and Hanna, G.L. (1998) 'Group Behavioural Therapy for Adolescents with Obsessive-Compulsive Disorder', *Research on Social Work Practice*, 8 (6): 629–36. This work involved externalising the problem; 11 of 15 participants providing follow-up data reported significant improvement after seven weeks.

Freeman, J., Epston, D. and Lobovits, D. (1997) *Playful Approaches to Serious Problems* (New York and London: Norton), pp. 112–3, reports on research undertaken by White and Epston into the effectiveness of letters to clients. Responses indicate that one letter is equivalent to 4.5 sessions.

George, E., Iveson, C. and Ratner, H. (1990) *Problem to Solution* (London: BT Press). Of 62 clients traced, 41 expressed satisfaction.

Johnson, L.D. and Shaha, S. (1996) 'Improving Quality in Psychotherapy', *Psychotherapy*, 33: 225–36. This study traced 38 clients who showed improvements in symptoms, relationships and social role after an average of 4.77 sessions.

Lindfoss, L. and Magnusson, D. (1997) 'Solution Focused Therapy in Prison', *Contempory Family Therapy*, 19: 89–104. A randomised study of 30 experimental and 29 controls were followed up at 16 and 20 months. 66 per cent of the experimental group re-offended, compared with 90 per cent of the control group, who also had more drug offences.

Macdonald, A. (1997) 'Brief Therapy in Adult Psychiatry: Further Outcomes', *Journal of Family Therapy*, 19: 213–22. After an average of 3.35 sessions, 12-month follow-up showed that 64 per cent of 36 clients had good outcomes. Long-standing problems did less well.

Nylund, D. and Tomas, J. (1994) 'The Economics of Narrative', *Family Therapy Networker*, 18 (6): 38–9, report that respondents rate the usefulness of narrative letters as equivalent to 3.2 sessions.

Wheeler, J. (1995) 'Believing in Miracles: The Implications and Possibilities of using Solution Focused Therapy in a Child Mental Health Setting', *ACPP Reviews and Newsletter*, 17: 255–61. A 3-month follow-up of 39 routine referrals and 34 solution-focused therapy referrals showed 44 per cent satisfaction in the first group and 68 per cent in the second.

Zimmerman, T.S., Prest, L.A. and Wetzel, B.E. (1997) 'Solution Focused Couples Therapy Groups: An Empirical Study', *Journal of Family Therapy*, 19: 127–44. 23 experimental groups compared favourably in outcomes with 13 controls on a Dyadic Adjustment Scale.

Appendix 2   Recommended
further reading

Milner, J. (2001) *Women and Social Work: Narrative Approaches* (Basingstoke: Palgrave).
Parton, N. and O'Byrne, P. (2000) *Constructive Social Work: Towards a New Practice* (Basingstoke: Macmillan – now Palgrave).
[These two books were written mainly for social workers but the first deals more fully with gender issues and the second deals more fully with constructionist theory than we do here.]

George, E., Iveson, C. and Ratner, H. (2000) *Problem to Solution*, (rev. edn) (London: BT Press).]
O'Connell, B. (1998) *Solution Focused Therapy* (London: Sage).
Hawkes, D., Marsh. T.I. and Wilgosh, R. (1998) *Solution-focused Therapy: A Handbook for Health Care Professionals* (Oxford: Butterworth Heinemann).
[These are useful books on the solution-focused approach.]

Payne, M. (2000) *Narrative Therapy: An Introduction for Counsellors* (London: Sage).
[An impressive account of the narrative approach.]

We also recommend all the seminal works of de Shazer, Berg, Miller, Dolan, White and Epston shown in the bibliography.
The London Brief Therapy Practice offers courses and conferences, usually in London or Glasgow, on solution-focused and narrative practice: www.brieftherapy.org.uk

Appendix 3   Scales

The following scales are based mainly on the ideas of Yvonne Dolan, Ron Kral and Eve Lipchik. The original versions of 3a, 3b and 3c were developed in Milner's work and published in Parton and O'Byrne (2000). 3d and 3e have been developed by us more recently, and 3f is also from Parton and O'Byrne whose version was based, with permission, on Kral's Solution Identification Scale.

Notes: The headings are expressed as competencies, e.g. 'tells the truth' rather than deficits. This aids exception-finding as rarely does a person tick all the 'not at all' boxes.

   Having numerous headings helps to give a balanced picture, where strengths are clearly shown in such a way that the client is empowered to tackle headings that get a left column tick. Ticking can be done by clients, their counsellors or others whose views the client might find useful. It can be helpful to complete a scale early in counselling and again later, for comparison.

3a   Survival of poor parenting scale

No.	Tick the box that fits best	Not at all	Just a little	Pretty much	Very much
1	Able to talk about what happened				
2	Able to talk about other things				
3	Able to grieve about what happened				
4	Able to cope with guilt about what happened				
5	Able to express anger about what happened				
6	Feels part of a new family				
7	Stands up for self				
8	Sleeps well				
9	Eats well				
10	Keeps smart				
11	Goes to social events				
12	Copes with new situations				
13	Meets new friends				
14	Laughs				
15	Able to choose supportive relationships				
16	Able to relax				
17	Able to tolerate criticism				
18	Able to accept praise				
19	Interested in the future				
20	Likes self				
21	Goes to school/work				
22	Other comments:				

3b Recovery scale for starting a new life after abuse

No.	Tick the box that fits best	Date: Not at all	Just a little	Pretty much	Very much
1	Able to talk about what happened				
2	Able to talk about other things				
3	Sleeps well				
4	Feels part of the family				
5	Stands up for self				
6	Keeps smart				
7	Goes to school/work				
8	Able to leave home				
9	Goes to social events				
10	Cares for relatives				
11	Eats well				
12	Copes with new situations				
13	Meets new friends				
14	Laughs				
15	Able to look male relatives in the eye				
16	Able to look male strangers in the eye				
17	Able to shake hands with male relatives				
18	Able to hold hands with male relatives				
19	Kisses male relatives				
20	Interested in the future				
21	Takes safety measures				
22	Chooses supportive relationships				
23	Able to relax				
24	Tolerates criticism				
25	Accepts praise				
26	Resists self-harm				

3c   Scale for reclaiming life after drugs

No.	Tick the box that fits best	Not at all	Just a little	Pretty much	Very much
		Date:			
1	Able to talk about the situation				
2	Able to talk about other things				
3	Likes him/herself				
4	Able to express anger about the past				
5	Able to make decisions				
6	Interested in the future				
7	Sleeps OK				
8	Shakes hands with confidence				
9	Takes safety measures				
10	Chooses supportive relationships				
11	Relaxes				
12	Accepts criticism				
13	Accepts praise				
14	Feels part of a family				
15	Stands up for him/herself				
16	Keeps smart				
17	Goes to work or school				
18	Goes to social events				
19	Cares for relatives				
20	Eats well				
21	Copes with new situations				
22	Meets new friends				
23	Laughs				
24	Has his/her own thoughts				
25	Feels in control				

3d   Overcoming violence scale

No.	Tick the box that fits best	Not at all	Just a time	Pretty much	Very much
1	I can talk calmly when I argue				
2	I can listen to my partner without interrupting				
3	I have a method to ensure we take turns				
4	I can accept that she has a right to be upset				
5	I feel appreciated and cared for by my partner				
6	When she is upset, I wait for her to calm down				
7	I do not use 'put-downs'				
8	If she puts me down, I have a planned response				
9	We respect each other's opinions				
10	We trust each other				
11	I can resist using sarcasm in arguments				
12	We can be honest with each other without fear				
13	When I notice angry words starting I have a plan to prevent them				
14	I remember it is okay to *feel* angry, but not okay to *do* anger, including words				
15	I take responsibility for the harm I have done using violence				
16	I realise I have no right to use violence to get my own way				
17	I do not feel I need to win when I argue with my partner				
18	I have worked out where my attitudes and ideas that say violence is okay have come from				
19	I can challenge attitudes and words that support violence				
20	When we argue we are not afraid of either one of us losing control				
21	I have ways to make it easier for my partner to tell me what she thinks				
22	I have ways of handling frustration at work				
23	I can control my drinking				
24	I can resist taking drugs				
25	I can ask for what I want politely (not expecting mind-reading)				
26	I ask for help when I need it				
27	We regularly plan things to promote a violence-free relationship				
28					
29					
30					

3e   Scale for getting and keeping a girl-friend

No.	Qualities women look for in men	Not at all	Just a little	Pretty much	Very much
1	Keep clean and smart				
2	Take her out (not necessarily expensive places – walks are fine)				
3	Holding hands				
4	Spoken TO not AT				
5	Make her feel special (Good manners, small gifts, cards)				
6	Cuddles (not necessarily leading to sex)				
7	Joint responsibility for contraception				
8	Make her laugh				
9	Show you are interested in her				
10	Not looking at other women when out				
11	Not expecting sex when you come home drunk				
12	Treat her as an equal				
13	Shared decision-making				
14	Give compliments				
15	(Add your own ideas)				
16					
17					

3f Student strengths scale

Part 1

No.	Tick the box that fits best	Not at all	Just a little	Pretty much	Very much
1	I get on well with other students				
2	I get on well at home				
3	I get on well with friends				
4	I get on well with teachers				
5	I get on well with other adults				
6	I cooperate with the ideas of others				
7	I adapt well to new situations				
8	I get on with my school work				
9	I take lessons seriously				
10	I behave well with teachers				
11	I complete what I start				
12	I am considerate towards others				
13	I can pay attention for a whole lesson				
14	I react with a reasonable mood				
15	I follow school rules				
16	I settle disagreements peacefully				
17	I cope with frustration				
18	I respect the rights of others				
19	I respect the rights of teachers				
20	Basically I am happy				
21	I sleep OK				
22	I feel part of my family				
23	I stand up for myself without losing control				
24	I can accept fair criticism				
25	I feel accepted by other students				
26	I show a sense of fair play				
27	I cope well with distractions				
28	I accept responsibility for my mistakes				
29	I cooperate with authority				
30	I accept praise well				
31	I can think before I act				
32	I can control excitement				
33	I handle stress well				
34	I respect people				
35	I cope with the subjects I have to study				
36	I am truthful				
37	I have a good influence on my friends				
38	I can ask for help when I need it				
39	I am accountable for my behaviour				

Part 2

Give yourself points out of 10 for the following; 0 = the pits'; 10 = per-fect. For example put 1 if its really bad but not the pits; or put 9 if its really good but not perfect.

How happy I am
How confident I am about improving it
How determined I am to do something about it
How well I get on with people
How confident I am about improving it
How determined I am to do something about it
How well my school work is going
How confident I am about improving it
How determined I am to do something about it
How well-behaved I am
How confident I am about improving it
How determined I am to do something about it
How well I cope with my biggest problem
How confident I am about improving it
How determined I am to do something about it

[This scale is adapted from that in Parton and O'Byrne (2000), part 1 of which was based, with permission, on Ron Kral's Solution Identification Scale, as published in Durrant 1993.]

Bibliography

Adams-Westcott, J., Daffron, T.A. and Sterne, P. (1993) 'Escaping Victim Life Stories', in S. Gilligan and R. Price (eds), *Therapeutic Conversations* (New York and London: Norton).

BACP (2000) Website – British Association for Counselling and Psychotherapy.

Bandler, R. and Grinder, J. (1979) *Frogs into Princes* (Moab, Utah: Real People Press).

Beck, A.T. (1991) *Anxiety Disorders and Phobias: A Cognitive Perspective* (New York: Basic Books).

Berg, I.K. (1994) *Family Based Services* (New York and London: Norton).

Berg, I.K. and Miller, S. (1992) *Working with the Problem Drinker: A Solution-focussed Approach* (New York and London: Norton).

Berg, I.K. and Reuss, N.M. (1998) *Solutions Step by Step: A Substance Abuse Treatment Manual* (New York and London: Norton).

Bertolino, B. and O'Hanlon. W.H. (1999) *Invitation to Possibility Land* (Philadelphia: Brunner/Mazel).

Beyebach, M. and Carranza, V. E. (1997) 'Therapeutic Interaction and Drop Out; Measuring Relational Communication in Solution-Focused Therapy', *Journal of Family Therapy*, 19(2): 173–212.

Blyth, E. and Milner, J. (1997) *Social Work with Children, the Educational Perspective* (London: Longman).

Bowlby, J. (1988) *A Secure Base: Clinical Applications of Attachment Theory* (London: Routledge).

Bowlby, J. and Parkes, C.M. (1970) 'Separation and Loss Within the Family', in E.J. Anthony and C. Koupernik (eds), *Growing Pains of Attachment Theory and Research*, Monographs of the Society for Research in Child Development, 50(1): 3–35.

Bretherton, I. (1992) 'The Origins of Attachment Theory: J. Bowlby & M. Ainsworth', *Developmental Psychology*, 28(5): 759–75.

Bruner, J. (1990) *Acts of Meaning* (Cambridge, MA: Harvard University Press).

Buchanan, A. (1999) *What Works for Troubled Children? Family Support for Children with Emotional Behavioural Problems* (Wiltshire County Council: Barnardos).

Budman, S.H. and Gurman, A.S. (1988) *Alcoholism and Substance Abuse: Strategies for Clinical Intervention* (New York: Free Press).

Burton, S., Regan, L. and Kelly, L. (1989) *Supporting Women and Challenging Men. Lessons from the Domestic Violence Intervention Programme* (Bristol: The Policy Press).

Byng-Hall, J. (1985) 'The Family Script: A Useful Bridge between Theory and Practice', *Journal of Family Therapy*, 7: 301–5.

Cade, B. and O'Hanlon, B. (1993) *A Brief Guide to Brief Therapy* (New York and London: Norton).

Cecchin, G. (1987) 'Hypothesising, Circularity and Neutrality: An Invitation to Curiosity', *Family Process*, 26(4): 405–13.

Chapman, T. and Hough, M. (2001) *Evidence Based Practice. A Guide to Effective Practice* (London: Home Office Inspectorate of Probation).

Circirelli, V.G. (1989) 'Feelings of Attachment to Siblings and Well Being in Later Life', *Psychology and Aging*, 4: 211–16.

Circirelli, V.G. (1991) 'Attachment Theory in Old Age: Protection of the Attachment Figure', in K. Pillemer and K. McCartney (eds), *Parent-Child Relationships across the Life Course* (Hillsdale, N.Y.: Erlbaum).

Coale, H.W. (1998) *The Vulnerable Therapist* (New York and London: The Haworth Press).

Cooper, J.F. (1995) *A Primer of Brief Psychotherapy* (New York and London: Norton).

Crittenden, P.M. (1988) 'Disturbed Patterns of Relationships in Maltreating Families; the Role of Initial Representation Models', *Journal of Reproductive and Infant Psychology*, 6(3): 183–200.

Culley, S. and Wright, J. (1997) 'Brief Time-Limited Counselling', in S. Palmer (ed.) with G. McMahon, *Handbook of Counselling*, 2nd edn (New York and London: Routledge).

De Milo, A. (1990) *Awareness* (New York: Doubleday).

Denborough, D. (1996) 'Step by Step: Developing Respectful and Effective Ways of Working with Young Men to Reduce Violence', in C. McLean, M. White and C. White (eds), *Men's Ways of Being* (Boulder, CA.: Westview Press).

Dermer, S.B., Hemesath, C.W. and Russell, C.S. (1998) 'A Feminist Critique of Solution-Focused Therapy', *American Journal of Family Therapy*, 26: 239–50.

Derrida, J. (1978) *Writing and Difference* (Chicago: University of Chicago Press).

De Shazer, S. (1982) *Patterns of Brief Family Therapy* (New York and London: Norton).

De Shazer, S. (1985) *Keys to Solutions in Brief Therapy* (New York and London: Norton).

De Shazer, S. (1988) *Clues: Investigating Solutions in Brief Therapy* (New York and London: Norton).

De Shazer, S. (1991) *Putting Difference to Work* (New York and London: Norton).

De Shazer, S. (1993) 'Vive la Difference', in S. Gilligan and R. Price (eds), *Therapeutic Conversations* (New York and London: Norton).

De Shazer, S. (1994) *Words were Originally Magic* (New York and London: Norton).

De Shazer, S. (1997) *Coming Through the Ceiling* (videotape) (Milwaukee, WI: Brief Family Therapy Centre).

Dobash, R.E., Dobash, R.P., Cavanagh, K. and Lewis, R. (2000) *Changing Violent Men* (London: Sage).

Dobash, R.E., Dobash, R.P., Cavanagh, K. and Lewis, R. (1996) *Research Evaluation of Programmes for Violent Men* (Edinburgh: Scottish Office Research Unit).

Dolan, Y. (1991) *Resolving Child Abuse: Solution-Focused Therapy and Ericksonian Hypnosis for Adult Survivors* (New York and London: Norton).

Dolan, Y. (1997) 'I'll Start my Diet To-morrow: A Solution-Focused Approach to Weight Loss', *Contemporary Family Therapy*, 19(1): 41–9.

Dolan, Y. (1998a) *One Small Step; Moving beyond Trauma to a Life of Joy* (Watsonville, CA: Papier-Mache Press).

Dolan, Y. (1998b) *Beyond Survival: Living Well is the Best Revenge.* Brief Therapy Practice Conference, London.

Dryden, W. (1999) *Rational Emotive Behavioural Counselling Action* (London: Sage).

Dryden, W. and Fletham, C. (1994) *Developing the Practice of Counselling* (London: Sage).

Dryden, W. and Mytton, J. (1999) *Four Approaches to Counselling and Psychotherapy* (London: Routledge).

Dupper, D.R. (1998) 'An Alternative to Suspension for Middle School Youths with Behavioural Problems: Findings for a "School Survival" Group', *Research on Social Work Practice*, 8(3): 354–66.

Durrant, M. and Kowalski, K. (1990) 'Overcoming the Effects of Sexual Abuse: Developing a Self-Perception of Competence', in M. Durrant and C. White (eds), *Ideas for Therapy with Sexual Abuse* (Adelaide: Dulwich Centre Publications).

Durrant, M. (1993) *Creative Strategies for School Problems* (Epping, NSW Aust.: Eastwood Family Therapy Centre).

Egan, G. (1998) *The Skilled Helper* (Monterey, CA: Brooks/Cole).

Elliott, H. (1997) 'Engendering Distinction: Postmodernism, Feminism and Narrative Therapy', *Gecko. Journal of Deconstruction and Narrative Ideas in Therapeutic Practice*, 1(5): 52–71.

Ellis, A. (1999) *How To Make Yourself Happy* (Atascadero, CA: Impact).

Epston, D. (1998) *Catching up with David Epston: A Collection of Narrative-based Papers, 1991–1996* (Adelaide: Dulwich Centre Publications).

Erikson, E.H. (1977) *Children and Society* (London: Granada).

Feeney, J. and Noller, P. (1996) *Adult Attachment* (London: Sage).

Feltham, C. (1996) *Time-limited Counselling* (London: Sage).

Foucault, M. (1972) *The Archaeology of Knowledge and the Discourse of Language* (New York: Pantheon).

Foucault, M. (1973) *The Birth of the Clinic* (London: Tavistock).

Foucault, M. (1980) *Power (Knowledge)* (New York: Pantheon).

Foucault, M. (1984) *Space, Knowledge and Power* (New York: Pantheon).

Foucault, M. (1988) 'Technologies of Self', in L. Martin, H. Gutman and P. Hutton (eds), *Technologies of the Self* (Amherst: University of Massachusetts Press).

Frankl, V.E. (1984) *Man's Search for Meaning* (New York: Touchstone Press).

Freeman, J., Epston, D. and Lobovits, D. (1997) *Playful Approaches to Serious Problems* (New York and London: Norton).

Furman, B. (1999) *Kids n' Skills: A Co-operative Educational Programme for Helping Children with Behavioural Problems.* Personal website.

Furman, B. and Ahola, T. (1992) *Solution Talk: Hosting Therapeutic Conversations* (New York and London: Norton).

Garfield, S.L. (1989) *The Practice of Brief Psychotherapy* (New York: Pergamon Press).

Garland, H.B. (1976) *Schiller* (Westport, Conn.: Greenwood Press).

Gibson, A. and Barrow, J. (1986) *The Unequal Struggle* (London: CCS Publications).

Gilgun, J.F. (1999) 'Mapping Resilience as Process among Adults with Childhood Adversities', in H.I. McCubbin, E.A. Thompson, A.I. Thompson and J.A. Futrell (eds), *The Dynamics of Resilient Families* (London: Sage).

Gilligan, C. (1982) *In a Different Voice: Psychological Theory and Women's Development* (Cambridge: Harvard University Press).

Graddol, D. and Swann, J. (1989) *Gender Voices* (Oxford: Blackwell).

Gullo, S.B. (1995) *Thin Tastes Better* (New York: Dell).

Gurman, A.S. (1977) 'Therapist and Patient Factors Influencing the Patient's Perception of Facilitative Therapeutic Conditions', *Psychiatry*, 40: 16–24.

Haley, J. (1997) *Leaving Home* (Philadelphia: Brunner/Mazel).

Halliday, M.A.K. (1978) 'Antileagues', in M.A.K. Halliday (ed), *Language as Social Semiotic: The Social Interpretation of Language and Meaning* (London: Arnold).

Harris, T. (1991) 'Getting Off the Conveyer Belt from Childhood Adversity: What We Can Learn from Naturalistic Studies', Paper presented at *Surviving Childhood Adversity*, 2–5 July (Dublin: Trinity College).

Hawkes, D., Marsh. T.I. and Wilgosh, R. (1998) *Solution Focused Therapy: A Handbook for Health Care Professionals* (Oxford: Butterworth Heinemann).

Holme, H. (2000) *Incest Group Therapy from a Systemic Solution Focused Perspective*, Paper presented at the European Brief Therapy Association conference, 25–27 August, Turku, Finland).

Horrocks, C. and Milner, J. (1999) 'The Residential Home as Serial Step-Family: Acknowledging Quasi-Sibling Relationships in Local Authority Residential Care', in A. Mullender (ed.), *We are Family, Siblings Relationships in Placement and Beyond* (London: British Agency for Adoption and Fostering).

Hudson, P. and O'Hanlon, W. (1991) *Rewriting Love Stories* (New York and London: Norton).

Ingleby, D. (1985) 'Professionals as Socialisers: The "Psy Complex"', in S. Spitz and A.T. Scull (eds) *Research in Law, Deviance and Social Control* (New York: Jai Press).

Iveson, C. (1990) *Whose Life? Community care of Older People and their Families* (London: Brief Therapy Press).

Jacob, F. (2001) '*Solution Focused Recovery from Eating Disorders* (London: BT Press).

Jenkins, A. (1990) *Invitations to Responsibility* (Adelaide: Dulwich Centre Publications).

Kahn, M. (1997) *Between Therapist and Client: The New Relationship*, revd edn (New York: Freeman & Co.).

Kaplan, A.G. (1992) 'When All is Said and Done; What is the Core of Brief Therapy?' *The Counselling Psychologist*, 20(3): 460–3.

Katz, I. (1996) *The Construction of Racial Identity in Children of Mixed Parentage: Mixed Metaphors* (London and Bristol, Pennsylvania: Jessica Kingsley).

Kowalski, K. (1990) 'The Girl with the Know-how; Finding Solutions to a School Problem', *Family Therapy Case Studies*, 5(1): 3–14.

Kral, R. (1989) *Strategies that Work: Techniques for Solutions in the Schools* (Milwaukee, WI: Brief Family Therapy Centre).

LaFontain, B., Garner, N. and Eliason, G. (1999) *Solution-Focused Counselling Groups: A Key for School Counsellors*, Internet http:// www. Ezonline.com/ grafton/solutions.html.

Letham, J. (1994) *Moved to Tears, Moved to Action. Solution Focused Brief Therapy with Women* (London: BT Press).

Leventhal, B. and Lundy, S.E. (eds) (1999) *Same-sex Domestic Violence. Strategies for Change* (London: Sage).

Lipchik, E. (1988) '*Purposeful Sequences for Beginning the Solution-Focused Interview*', in E. Lipchik (ed.), *Interviewing* (Rockville, MD: Aspen).

Macdonald, A. (1997) 'Brief Therapy in Adult Psychiatry – Further Outcomes', *Journal of Family Therapy*, 19(2): 213–22.

Madge, N. (1997) *Abuse and Survival: A File* (London: The Prince's Trust, in association with National Children's Bureau).

Mander, G. (2000) *Psychodynamic Approach to Brief Therapy* (London: Sage).

Manthei, R. (1997) *Counselling: The Skills of Finding Solutions to Problems* (London: Routledge).

Marlatt, G.A. and Gordan, J. (eds) (1985) *Relapse Prevention* (New York: Guilford).

Marvin, R.S. and Stewart, R.S.A. (1990) 'A Family System Framework for the Study of Attachment', in M. Greenberg, D. Cichetti and M. Cummings (eds), *Attachment beyond the Pre-school Years* (Chicago: University of Chicago Press).

Maslow, A.A. (1954) *Motivation and Personality* (New York: Harper & Row).

Masson, J. (1989) *Against Therapy* (London: Fontana).

Maturana, H. (1988) 'The Search for Objectivity or the Request for a Compelling Argument', *Irish Journal of Psychology*, 9: 25–82.

McFarland, B. (1995) *Brief Therapy and Eating Disorders* (San Francisco: Jossey-Bass Wiley).

McLeod, J. (1997) *Narrative and Psychotherapy* (London: Sage).

Mearns, D. (1994) *Developing Person-Centred Counselling* (London: Sage).

Mearns, D. and Thorne, B. (1999) *Person-Centred Counselling in Action*, 2nd edn (London: Sage).

Messerschmidt, S.W. (2000) *Nine Lives. Adolescent Masculinities, The Body and Violence* (Boulder, Col.: Westview Press).

Miller, G. (1997a) *Becoming Miracle Workers: Language and Meaning in Brief Therapy* (New York: Aldine de Gruyter).

Miller, G. (1997b) 'Systems and Solutions: The Discourses of Brief Therapy', *Contemporary Family Therapy*, 19: 5–22.

Miller, S.D., Duncan, B.L. and Hubble, M.A. (1996) *Handbook of Solution-Focussed Brief Therapy* (San francisco: Jossey-Bass).

Miller, S.D., Duncan, B.L. and Hubble, M.A. (1997) *Escape from Babel: Toward a Unifying Language of Psychotherapy Practice* (New York and London: Norton).

Milner, J. (1993) 'A Disappearing Act: The Differing Career Paths of Fathers and Mothers in Child Protection Investigations', *Critical Social Policy*, 38(3): 48–68.

Milner, J. (2001) *Women and Social Work: Narrative Approaches* (Basingstoke: Palgrave).

Molnar, A. and Lindquist, B. (1989) *Changing Problem Behaviours in Schools* (San Francisco: Jossey-Bass).
Morrow, S.W. and Hawxhurst, D.M. (1998) 'Lesbian Partner Abuse. Implication for Therapists' *Journal of Counselling and Development* 68: 58–62.
Murphy, J. (1992) 'Brief Strategic Family Intervention for School-Related Problems', *Family Therapy Case Studies*, 5(1): 61–74.
Murphy, K. (1996) 'Men and Offending Groups', in T. Newburn and A. Mair (eds), *Working with Men* (Lyme Regis: Russell House Publishing).
Neimeyer, G.J. (ed.) (1993) *Constructivist Assessment* (New York: Sage).
Noonan, E. (1983) *Counselling Young People* (London: Methuen).
O'Connell, B. (1998) *Solution-Focused Therapy* (London: Sage).
O'Hanlon, B. (1993) 'Possibility Therapy', in S. Gilligan and R. Price (eds), *Therapeutic Conversations* (New York and London: Norton).
O'Hanlon, B. (1995) *Breaking the Bad Trance*. London conference ('Breaking the Bad Trance').
O'Hanlon, W.H. and Weiner-Davis, M. (1989) *In Search of Solutions* (New York and London: Norton).
Parkes, C.M. (1972) *Bereavement: Studies of Grief in Adult Life* (New York: International Universities Press).
Parton, N. and O'Byrne, P. (2000) *Constructive Social Work: Towards a New Practice* (Basingstoke: Macmillan – now Palgrave).
Payne, M. (2000) *Narrative Therapy: An Introduction for Counsellors* (London: Sage).
Peake, A. and Fletcher, M. (1997) *Strong Mothers. A Resource for Mothers and Carers of Children who have been Sexually Abused* (Lyme Regis: Russell House Publishing).
Perlman, H.H. (1979) *Relationship: The Heart of Helping People* (Chicago: University of Chicago Press).
Phillips, A. (1993) *On Kissing, Tickling and Being Bored* (London: Faber & Faber).
Price, R. (1993) 'If You Really Knew Me: An Exploration of Therapeutic Concerns in Collaborating with the "Damaged" Self', in S. Gilligan and R. Price (eds), *Therapeutic Conversations* (New York and London: Norton).
Radke-Yarrow, M., Cummings, E.M. and Kuvcinsky, L. (1985) 'Patterns of Attachment in Two- and Three-Year-Olds in Normal Families and Families with Parental Depression', *Child Development*, 56: 884–93.
Reeves, R. (2001) *Happy Mondays: Putting The Pleasure Back Into Work* (London: Pearson Education).
Renzetti, C.M. (1992) *Violent Betrayal. Partner Abuse in Lesbian Relationship* (London: Sage).
Rich, A. (1977) *Of Woman Born, Motherhood as Institution and Experience* (London: Virago).
Rogers, C. (1951) *Client-Centered Therapy* (London: Constable).
Rogers, C. (1961) *On Becoming a Person* (London: Constable).
Selekman, M.D. (1997) *Solution-focused Therapy with Children* (New York and London: Guilford Press).
SFT e-mail list: contact www.enabling.org/ia/sft.
Smith, S., Cox, D. and Saradjian, J. (1998) *Women and Self-harm* (London: The Women's Press).
Sobell, M.B. and Sobell, L.C. (1978) *Behavioral Treatment of Alcohol Problems: Individualised Therapy and Controlled Drinking* (New York: Plenum).

Spacks, P.M. (1986) *Gossip* (Chicago and London: University of Chicago Press).

Spender, D. (1985) *Man Made Language*, 2nd edn (London: Routledge & Kegan Paul).

Stacey, K. (1997) 'Alternative Metaphors for Externalising Conversations', in *Gecko, Journal of Deconstruction and Narrative Ideas in Therapeutic Practice*, 1(5): 29–51.

Strand, P.S. (1997) 'Towards a Developmentally Informed Narrative Therapy', *Family Process*, 36: 329–39.

Talmon, M. (1990) *Single Session Therapy: Maximising the Effect of the First (and often only) Therapeutic Encounter* (San Francisco: Jossey-Bass).

Tamasese, K. and Waldegrave, C. (1996) 'Culture and Gender Accountability in the "Just Therapy" Approach', in C. McLean, M. Carey and C. White (eds), *Men's Ways of Being* (Colorado and Oxford: Westview Press).

Tomm, K. (1993) 'The Courage to Protest', in S. Gilligan and R. Price (eds), *Therapeutic Conversations* (New York and London: Norton).

Turnell, A. and Edwards, S. (1999) *Signs of Safety: A Solution and Safety Oriented Approach to Child Protection Casework* (New York and London: Norton).

Turnell, A. and Lipchik, E. (1999) 'The Role of Empathy in Brief Therapy: The Overlooked but Vital Context', *Australia and New Zealand Journal of Family Therapy*, 20(4): 177–82.

Waldrond Skinner, S. (1976) *Family Therapy: The Treatment of Natural Systems* (London: Routledge & Kegan Paul).

Wallerstein, R.S. (1989) 'The Psychotherapy Research Project on the Menninger Foundation: An overview', *Journal of Consulting and Clinical Psychology*, 57(2): 195–205.

Wallerstein, J.S. and Blakesee, S. (1996) *The Good Marriage, How and Why Love Lasts* (London: Bantam).

Walsh, F. (1999) 'Partner Abuse' in Davies, D. and Neal, C. *Pink Therapy. A Guide for Counsellors and Therapists working with Lesbian, Gay and Bi-sexual Clients* (Buckingham and Philadelphia: Open University Press).

Walters, M. (1988) *The Invisible Web: Gender Patterns in Family Relationships* (New York: Guilford Press).

Weakland, J. (1993) 'Conversation, but What Kind?', in S. Gilligan and R. Price (eds), *Therapeutic Conversations* (New York and London: Norton).

Weingarten, K. (1998) 'The Small and the Ordinary: The Daily Practice of a Postmodern Narrative Therapy, *Family Process*, 37: 3–15.

Weiss, R.S. (1973) *Loneliness: The Experience of Emotional and Social Isolation* (Cambridge, MA: MIT Press).

Wheeler, J. (1995) 'Believing in Miracles: The Implication of Using Solution-Focused Therapy in a Child Mental Health Setting', *ACPP Review and Newsletter*, 17(5): 249–54.

White, M. (1984) 'Pseudo-Encopresis: From Avalanche to Victory, From Vicious to Victorious Circles', *Family Systems Medicine*, 2(2): 150–60.

White, M. (1993) 'Deconstruction and Therapy', in S. Gilligan and R. Price (eds), *Therapeutic Conversations* (New York and London: Norton).

White, M. (1995) *Re-authoring Lives: Interviews and Essays* (Adelaide: Dulwich Centre Publications).

White, M. (1996) *Narrative Practice*, Doncaster conference.

White, M. and Epston, D. (1990) *Narrative Means to Therapeutic Ends* (New York and London: Norton).

Williams, F. (1993) 'Women and Community', in J. Bornat, C. Pereira, D. Pilgrim and F. Williams (eds), *Community Care; A Reader* (Basingstoke: Macmillan – now Palgrave).

Winslade, J. and Monk, G. (2000) *Narrative Mediation: A New Approach to Conflict Resolution* (San Francisco, CA: Jossey-Bass).

Wittgenstein, L. (1963) *Philosophical Investigations*, 3rd edn (Oxford: Blackwell).

Woolfe, R. (1997) 'Counselling in Britain: Present Position and Future Prospects', in S. Palmer and G. McMahon (eds), *Handbook of Counselling*, 2nd edn (New York and London: Routledge).

Index